STILL AFLOAT

AFLOAT

150 YEARS OF EXETER ROWING CLUB

By Alan Peacock

Published in the UK by Imprint Academic
PO Box 200, Exeter EX5 5YX, UK

ISBN 9 781845 407636

A CIP catalogue record for this book is available from the
British Library

CONTENTS

THANKS, ACKNOWLEDGEMENTS AND APOLOGIES

MANY THANKS go to all the following people, without whom the book could never have been produced:

Bethan Lewis, for masterminding the whole project and for searching through a mountain of old photographs

Ros and Brian Sculpher, Kirstin Martin, Margaret Burgess, Ray Grigg and **Tim Spencer**, for their tireless research and the mountain of information and ideas they provided

Brian Penn for taking many excellent photos

Lucinda Sanders for faultless proof-reading and typesetting

Keith Sutherland at *Imprint,* for efficiently producing the final volume, and for their generosity towards the venture

Dan Rowse for the up to date inventory of our boats

All those who gave their time to write contributions, to be interviewed or to dig out old photographs, newsletters and memorabilia including (in alphabetical order), **Paula Bowden, Sue and Dave Brooks, Eleanor Burke, Annette Dentith, Kevin Dentith, Ray Grigg, Denzil & Wyn Hitt, Hana Lango-Allen, Dave Parsons, Stuart Redden, Chris Rogers, Brian Sculpher, Paul Wilson, Julia Wood.**

And we offer our **apologies** to anyone who feels their contribution has been overlooked or diminished in any way. Hundreds if not thousands of people have contributed to the success of the club; acres of documentation have been sifted through to put the book together. If there are errors and omissions, the responsibility for these lies solely with the author, not the many contributors, to whom go my thanks.

EXETER IN THE 1860s

In early 2013, posters could be seen in London stations saying '*Invest in Exeter*', pointing out that our city had 'College of the Year, University of the Year and Museum of the Year'. And since the arrival of investments like the new Met Office, John Lewis, Princesshay, Cranbrook, the Business Park, Science Park and Skypark, Sandy Park, extensive residences for students, new hotels, and the Haven Banks Outdoor Education centre' , plus the forthcoming IKEA store and rugby World Cup, Exeter has definitely been on the up, in many ways bucking the recession which has hit much of the country hard in recent years.

But back in the 1860s, the reverse was true. A few decades earlier, Exeter had been the sixth largest town in England, and the fourth largest port: so important that the Tsar of Russia sent his son to Topsham to study as a shipwright, as Topsham was seen as second only to London as a base for shipbuilding. But Exeter had been slowly overhauled by industrial towns in the north and midlands, so that by the 1860s it was only the 60th in size, with a population about one quarter of what it is today.

Exe Island was the early industrial area of Exeter, an area of marshland between the city walls and the River Exe, reclaimed by the construction of a series of leats or water courses, possibly from as early as the 10th century. Of these, the Higher Leat, which leaves the river near the Mill on the Exe, still exists, though much of it is now culverted. It flows back into the river below Cricklepit Bridge, and created Exe Island, which was a separate manor belonging to the Courtenays, Earls of Devon.

The leats were used to drive fulling mills and corn mills. Sometime between 1180 and 1190 Robert Courtenay granted to Nicholas Gervaise 'all his water which Thomas the fuller holds of him outside the west gate of Exeter, which is between his corn mills and Crickenpette, so that the said Nicholas and his heirs may build a mill on the said water towards Crickenpette as shall appear best and most commodious to them'.

There is also evidence for other medieval industries—tanning and the working of horn, bone, and bronze— which has come to light in archaeological excavations. Cloth-finishing was the most important industry in the 16th century. In the late 18th century, the cloth industry declined and in the 19th century the area was occupied by iron foundries, corn mills, and breweries.

There were three main reasons for this industrial decline. First of all, the wool trade on which Exeter's wealth had been built was declining in importance. Secondly, the industrial revolution that was expanding the northern cities so fast depended on steam power; but Exeter was too far from sources of coal to make a manufacturing industry economically viable. And the third and final nail in the coffin, as far as the port and its maritime trade was concerned, was the coming of the railway to Exeter in 1844. Suddenly, sending freight by rail was quicker and cheaper than by ship, and the role of the port declined.

In the years leading up to 1860, Exeter had not been a happy place. The city still faced very serious problems of disease and poverty: the shock of the cholera outbreak of a few years earlier was still in many people's minds and the work of the Improvement Commissioners to improve sanitation was far from complete. The Exeter Food Riots in 1847 and again in 1854, when residents stormed the market demanding affordable prices for food, had hit the national headlines. The rapid decline in trade and income for the canal threatened its bankruptcy: revenues had fallen by over half in a few years. The recently concluded Crimean War, the first to be extensively reported and photographed, had brought discord across the country.

Public health was a major problem, not only in Exeter but nationally. In 1864, The London Times reported that the stench from the river Thames was so unbearable that Parliament was unable to operate. At that time, only surface water was removed through sewage systems: human waste simply accumulated in cess pools which, according to the same letter in the Times, 'riddled basements and gave forth deadly gases which filled houses and killed us with fevers'. The same letter, from a large group of Lords and MPs, urged sewers to be constructed to deal with waste and prevent rivers from progressive pollution.

In Exeter, the problem was just as bad. What is now Paris Street was then known as Shitbrook Street, as it led down to the Shitbrook, a stinking drain carrying human waste that flowed across what is now Barnfield Road, past Bull Meadow and Larkbeare House, to enter the river close to the Port Royal; which in that same year was where Exeter Rowing Club was founded! So there's a good chance that many of the boats were rowing in what was not much better than an open sewer at the time. And it may be no coincidence that, in *Trewman's Exeter Flying Post,* a local newssheet of the time, the March 6th issue of 1864 printed an advert from a Dr. Barry claiming that:

> 'all nervous, liver and stomach complaints in every stage
> are perfectly curable by [my] health restoring Revalenta
> Arabica food, as proved by thousands of cases which had
> been considered hopeless'.

Did rowers in that early club experience stomach problems and test his remedy, perhaps?!

Fortunately, only three years later in 1867, Lister invented antiseptics and thus began the process of tackling health problems which up to then had killed thousands. Yet as late as 1912, the Devon and Exeter Gazette reported on

> "the Unsatisfactory state of River Exe - It is a serious
> Indictment that from Cowley Bridge to Countess Wear the
> river is nothing more nor less than a series of open
> cesspools."

Disease was compounded by poverty and the appalling slums in Exeter's west quarter at the time. In 1854, as the local press reported,

> 'people in Exeter and Taunton and some other towns in
> the west of England had proceeded to the markets, and
> compelled the dealers in provisions, both corn and meat, to
> sell them at such prices as those bodies of people chose to
> fix'...

This was the start of what became called the Food Riots, after which a large number of rioters were sent to trial and 44 were convicted. 'The mob' it was claimed by the press, 'was clearly incited by women,' and attributed this to their 'great ignorance and the excitement produced by intoxicating drink'.

And yet while the river was still polluted, landowners were investing in salmon stocking and breeding in the Exe. At Tiverton in 1864, 60,000 salmon par and 40,000 'white trout' par were introduced from Galway, with the intention that 'in every probability, the Exe would be well stocked with salmon in 3 or 4 years'. The salmon fishery continues to this day; though then as now, few local people were able to benefit from eating the expensive fish, unless they were successful poachers.

Exeter's trade was at this time dependent on the canal, which had been completed and opened in 1827, to allow large ships into the port of Exeter. When traffic declined in the 1860s, due to the arrival of the railway, a plan was made to enable goods to be despatched by rail from the canal basin, though nothing seems to have come of this. There was intense competition between boatmen in Exeter and Topsham to carry goods up and down the canal, and this may go some way to explaining why young men wanted not only to row but also to be better and faster than their rivals in the other port, thus prompting them to start a rowing club. In fact, competitive rowing was recorded as early as 1846, when Isca (Exeter) Club's four won the Dove Cup at Teignmouth Regatta.

The 1860s, as you can see, were turning out to be a turbulent decade. In 1861, Prince Albert, the Queen's consort, died of typhoid, and Victoria went into permanent mourning. The Prime Minister at the time was Viscount Palmerston, who had founded the Liberal party; he had ended the Crimean war, which had been badly managed and left the problems in the Balkans unresolved, but this didn't prevent him taking Britain to war again, first in Hong Kong and then in attempting to put down the Indian Mutiny. But his real headache was in America, where the abolition of slavery had led to the breakdown of the Slave Trade, already suffering from the abolition of slavery in most of Europe. This led to the American civil war between the Confederacy of the South and the Northern states, bringing about death and the destruction on a large scale, the first modern war in effect.

Despite this, Palmerston was a popular Prime Minister, and was re-elected with a large majority in 1865, but he died before he could form a new government. People and political parties were so divided that Britain had no less than four Prime Ministers in the next four years; Earl Russell (for one year), Lord Derby (two years), Benjamin Disraeli (a few weeks) and William Gladstone, who final gave some stability to national politics in 1868.

Exeter meanwhile had a popular Liberal MP, a Mr. Divett, who had been returned unopposed for many years, but who died in 1864. The Conservatives were expected to win the by-election easily, as their candidate, Lord Courtenay, had the support of the county aristocracy. But at the election, he managed to scrape through by only 1,096 votes to 1,070 (about the same turnout as for a large Exeter City Council ward today!) prompting some at the meeting to turn angry. The press reported that Lord Courtenay

> *'essayed to address the meeting but sat down after two or three ineffectual attempts to obtain a hearing'.*

Not a good start!

The Port Royal, a building that had been through several changes of use, was the first base for the club. It had originally been two cottages near the lime kilns, and is first mentioned in 1823 when the wife of the landlord of the Fountain Inn (now the Prospect Inn) was found in the river nearby. She was taken to what was called The Exeter Humane Society, 'near the Lime Kilns', which probably was one of the buildings that became the Port Royal, but never recovered.

Photo 1: Port Royal 1869

It began trading as a public house in 1844, when Robert Ugler is listed as the landlord of the Port Royal Tavern, and was taken over in 1850 by a George Webber, who was then 'running the Port Royal at St. Leonard's Quay'. Five years later, the *Exeter Journal and Almanack* listed John Western as landlord, followed in 1857 by Charles Edwards. He was just 26 years old at the time, the son of the ferryman at the quay who ran a passage-boat and who was also a boat builder. His mother continued to run the ferry after her husband's death; when she died in 1877, Charles wrote to the council offering to continue running the ferry at the same rent as his late mother, £100 a year. However, though the lease was put out to tender, it is not known who the next ferryman was. But Charles Edwards was landlord at the Port Royal when the Rowing Club was founded.

There have in fact been six rowing clubs in Exeter at different times. Isca Rowing Club, which became Exeter Amateur Rowing Club in 1864, existed as early as 1846, according to records. In 1893, the St. Thomas Rowing Club was formed, but this was disbanded in 1921. The University, then the University College of the South West, had a rowing club before WW2; and in 1927, the Port Royal Amateur Rowing Club was formed. The PRARC amalgamated with Exeter Rowing Club in 1946, probably due to the fact that both clubs were suffering from a lack of members, funds and serviceable boats after the war. The newly-formed Exeter Rowing Club had its first regatta on the river in 1946, racing from Bonhay Weir (by the Mill on the Exe pub) to the Port Royal.

It was also in this year that St. Luke's College (now part of the University) formed a boat club, and used the ERC boats to train its students. Since then, the ERC and the University have at various times collaborated through lending each other boats for example, and in recent years the 'Varsity Regatta' between the two clubs has proved popular.

So the Exeter Rowing Club has a rich history. There have been ups and downs, good times and bad, successes and disappointments, and some very strange incidents. We hope that the information and stories collected in the following chapters, as well as the names of prominent and often well-loved personalities, will hold your interest to the end, where in 2014 the club is thriving.

THE FIRST 50 YEARS

"The first years of the existence of the Exeter Amateur Rowing Club are, to borrow from a scribe older than myself, shrouded in the mists of antiquity"....

These words opened the *'Short Rowing History of the E.A.R.C'* by E.H. Dart, one of the sources on which this book is based. We have also drawn heavily on another document, *'History of the club from its formation in 1864'* by A.B.Edwards. But most of all, the information and the stories below would not have been possible without the painstaking research work of Ros Sculpher, Kirstin Martin and others who have slaved away at the Heritage Centre, working their way through boxes and boxes of old documents about the club.

Photo 1: Mr E H Dart

Most of the book is organised by themes- boats, people, competitions, successes, social events etc- so as to make it more interesting to read. This chapter simply tries to give a flavour of how the club started, who were the key people involved in establishing the club, and how it progressed up to the time of the Great War (WW1).

"One may safely say" claims Mr. Dart, *"that our first rowing man was the man who is also its founder- 'Dick' Southcott, as his contemporaries affectionately styled him"*. Mr. Richard Southcott was from the well-known firm of Southcott and Honey, who provided the club in 1868 with its first four-oared boat for £20 (a price that would not buy even a single oar now!). Southcott and a select circle of his friends set about the task of forming an Athletic Rowing Club with the object of encouraging rowing as a sport, a task at which they clearly succeeded, as the club has survived for 150 years.

The four-oared boat was not, however the club's first boat. In 1864, the club purchased an eight named *'St John of Malta'* from a Mr. E. Follwell, the first secretary of the club, a boat that the club used for the

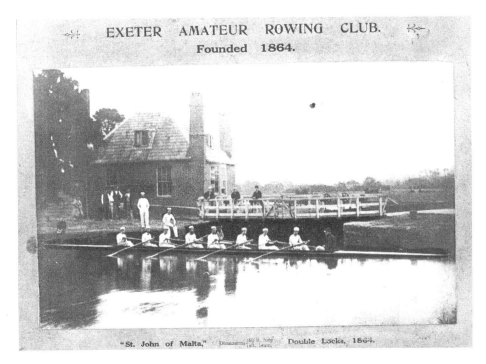

EXETER AMATEUR ROWING CLUB.
Founded 1864.

"St. John of Malta," Dimensions Double Locks, 1864.

Photo 2: St John of Malta at Double Locks 1864 with original crew of T. Guscott; W. Henderson; H. Beck; N. O'Leary; H.J. Dicker; W. Weicht; F. Sprague; G.Madge. Cox: E. Fullwell

next 13 years before it was broken up.

They were however very proud of this boat, and had the outriggers gilded in 1865. It was because of the boat's name that the club adopted the Maltese cross as its emblem, and this appeared on the club uniform for many years, which was a white vest and sweater with a blue Maltese cross. The original club uniform also included a straw hat with blue band and white Maltese cross, as well as a blue blazer with white braiding and Maltese cross. There were several attempts over the years to replace this uniform; one proposal, in 1893, was to race in pink, green and apricot! This clearly didn't catch on, though.

Club membership in the first year consisted of 21 people (all men of course, in those days) who each paid 15s 6d (77p) in membership fees. The club's first Annual Dinner that year was attended by 41 people; and in 1865, membership rose to 38, when three boats were bought from Bristol, though records don't show what kind these were or who built them. These original members were obviously tremendously fond of their sport, as for the first four years they kept the club going just for the love of it; little money was available, so equipment was paid for by the

Photo 3: Open day 1908 with the club uniform

members, out of their own pockets it seems. As a result of having few boats- one eight, one four, for example- there was not much opportunity to indulge in competitive rowing. Members arranged races against each other, and occasionally against other local men and professionals, in whatever boats were available, or which could be hired. Eventually, some members tired of this and formed their own club, called 'Exonia Club', which seemed discouraging at the time, but actually proved to be a blessing in disguise, as it led to serious competition between the clubs and brought on a real strain of successful rowers.

In 1868, a Mr. George Ross and three friends were determined to obtain a four in which they might stand a chance of racing against other clubs. The boat, named '*Amateur*', was purchased from Plymouth for £20, the members contributing half of the cost, the club funds the other half. Mr Dart says that '*the boat was rigged the wrong way for turning, and because of this, many races were lost on our short course, simply because of the turns*'. This course, in the early days, ran from the weir on Bonhay Road down to the Port Royal, which was the first base of the club. A second boat, called *Psyche*, was also purchased, which proved to be much better, and some notable successes were achieved in this boat. This was important to the club, because by 1869, membership had dwindled to 20 and the membership fee reduced to 10s 6d (52p), probably to attract more members.

One early success was achieved in 1871 when a four rowed by Orchard, Norrington, Turner and Carter competed against a four from

Bristol, for four silver cups. After a very tight race, the Exeter boat was fouled and damaged coming round the bend at the quay. The foul was claimed and allowed, and the Exeter crew decided they would race again the same afternoon, if repairs could be done in time. A cabinet maker called Hayman managed to do the necessary work; the crews turned out and Exeter won the cups in the afternoon.

1871 was notable also because it was the year that paired boats were rowed without a cox for the first time. The club also introduced canoe races, which involved shooting Trew's Weir and carrying canoes over the fields to the canal, before canoeing to the winning post! And in the same year, two 'freshmen', Mr. Pike and Mr. Horsley, were recruited to make up a four, one of whom had just left the Exonia club. The pair proved to be almost invincible in pairs and skiffs, as well as in the four, and they continued racing well into the1880s. They were backed up by other stalwarts of the club, including Messrs. Edwards, Mason, Sewell, Smith and Lawless.

This was also the year of the famous trip made by an Exeter crew who rowed to Torquay in a four, and back to Dawlish in the same day, two of them eventually bringing the boat back across the Exe estuary in a half gale. At the time, Mr. Dart's view of what makes a good rower was as follows:

> *We must get to like working hard for our sport. The successful rowing man puts rowing first: he thinks of nothing else in his leisure hours, and regulates all his habits for the advantage of his hobby. Add to this plenty of practice and patience, and if a man can row at all, he will row well.*

Is this still true today?

Club matches became very competitive around this time. Some of the main competitors were the clubs from Starcross, Torquay, Totnes, Dartmouth, Bideford and Teignmouth, Starcross and Torquay being the strongest of these at the time. In 1879, the first junior members were recorded, with prizes offered at the regatta to Seniors and Juniors in fours, pairs and canoes. And it was not until 1883 that the term 'skiff' first appeared in the list of competitive races. The club had bought two skiffs, named *Southampton* and *Reply,* by 1873, but there were not enough such boats around to permit racing.

In 1880, the club undertook the organisation of the Exeter Regatta for the first time. The club also enhanced its good name by lending the four *'Psyche'* to the Torquay crew so that they could compete in Exeter, and in 1881, by loaning a boat to Plymouth so that they could compete at Bideford. But around 1883, competition seemed to fall flat, and in 1884 the racing did not seem to take place at all. Dart suggests that this may have been brought about by the sudden increase of interest amongst members in rowing the skiffs rather than the larger boats, as well as the frustrations felt by some people with the existing classification of boats. For several years, therefore, regattas seemed to have been abandoned, replaced by local club matches. Some members took advantage of this to lobby for the purchase of dinghies or 'Oxfords' as they were then called.

By 1886, however, records show that membership was back up to where it had been, thanks to 25 new members joining. New boats were purchased, and at the Annual Dinner, a testimonial was presented to Mr. Charles Richards, the boatman from the Port Royal, which had been the club's base since its foundation, for his 'kindness and courtesy to all members of the EARC'. Names associated with the club at this time were those that became familiar over the following years; Hannaford, Edwards, Edworthy, Mudge, Stagg, Lincoln, Pollard, Pring, Heath, Randall, Sandford, Hodge and others. Hannaford and Edwards in particular were known to be 'hard nuts to crack', and for several years they won skiff championships regularly. They were almost as 'hot', it was said, when rowing a pair. And it was about this time that racing in double skiffs was introduced.

In 1887, it was intended that Exeter should hold a regatta again, but the tragedy of the Exeter Theatre fire put this on hold; instead, the club donated £50 to the Fire Relief Fund. This was not the first theatre fire in Exeter; the old theatre in Bedford Square burned down in the 1820s. But the Great Theatre Fire of 1887 was the worst in English history. It has been described in the media as follows:

> *The Theatre Royal was built at the top of Longbrook Street with a capacity for 1,500, with little regard to fire safety - lessons had not been learned. The Exeter Theatre Company moved in during 1886. On the 5th September 1887, on the first night of a romantic comedy called Romany Rye, and with an audience of 800, a naked gas flame ignited some drapes. Within moments, panic broke out as the flames spread. Despite the valiant efforts of the West of England Insurance Co. fire brigade, using the "Little West" fire engine, the flames spread through the*

building.

Robert Pople, landlord of the New London Inn was quickly on the scene with ladders to rescue the audience. He used the inn to shelter the victims, and the stables to lay out the dead.

There were 186 victims, many from the upper gallery who could not escape because of poorly designed exits - many victims were suffocated in the crush. Most were buried in a mass grave in Higher Cemetery and a memorial cross carved by Harry Hems placed over the spot.

This disaster was the worst theatre fire in British history, and soon, Parliament legislated to bring in stringent safety precautions in all British theatres, including the fire proof safety curtain. Exeter also gained its first electricity generating station which supplied the newly installed electric lighting system in the new Theatre Royal.

However, the regatta was reintroduced in 1888, when club membership was up to 88 with a new four, the *Ormonde;* Exeter crews took first and second places. A feature of this regatta was the presence of a Mr. G. Bubear, the skiff champion, a man who seems to have made his living by going around challenging other rowers. He rowed against selected local scullers and a four, defeating everything he took on.

This was also the time when the club introduced the idea of 'Club Four' competitions, rather like the Georgie Fours that continue today. The club selected sixteen men to fill four boats; four were nominated as captains, and these drew names from a hat to make up their crews. Anyone refusing to row as drawn forfeited their entrance fee of half a crown (2s 6d, or about 12p). As Dart explains, this was '*hardly a perfect system to the minds of those who like to see a crew row well together, but one that must have occasioned much good sport'.* In one case, a crew with a man short still managed, with two oars on one side and one on the other, to win their race.

This seemed to be a successful period for the club, as several new boats were purchased and membership continued to rise. Members were still contributing considerably to the funding of the club, however; for example, until 1890, crews had to pay all expenses relating to the carriage and transport of boats to away regattas. Sadly, no records seem to be available of EARC's performance at these regattas in other parts of the region. But a good idea of the strength of the club at this time can be gathered from the programmes of the Exeter regatta from 1890-1898. The senior fours won two firsts and four seconds; junior fours two firsts and one third. Senior pairs won one first, five seconds and one third; while junior pairs won one first, two seconds and two thirds.

In 1892, the first Clasper-built four was purchased for £46 and named '*Spinaway*'. The firm of Clasper, Salter and Kessell of Plymouth built several boats for the club between 1880 and 1907, but it seems that the company no longer exists, so records of the particular boats are not available. Thirteen new members joined in 1892, and the club took part in the Exeter Carnival for the first time. Annual dinners were a regular feature of the social calendar, being held in such places as the White Hart and Shrimpton's Bude Hotel. The following year, 19 new members joined, taking the club up to 83 men and by 1896, another 25 new members joined, which meant that the club had to buy new skiffs; at least eight were purchased in these few years. The club also managed to keep in the red, if only just at times; records show that despite all the purchases, the club had a balance of £15 5s in 1897, when for the first time lockers were built into the dressing room at the Port Royal. The boatman there, a Mr. Richards, died after a long illness, and the club presented a testimonial for his long service.

However, what goes around comes around, as they say; and by 1899 membership began to decline again. The explanation offered by Mr. Edwards was that it was due to the rising popularity of cycling. His account claims that there was 'no active rowing spirit prevailing' in the club. By 1901, membership was down to 66. Still, a club picnic was held at double locks, and the club was notable for some interesting social events around this time as outlined in a later chapter. By 1902, the club decided for the first time not to charge entrance fees; a sure sign that there were problems, and this continued until 1906. Still, the club continued to buy new skiffs, and rules were revised to make membership more attractive. 1896 also saw the foundation of the West of England Amateur Rowing Association (WEARA) which has overseen competition in the region ever since.

This all seems to have worked to some extent, because in 1903 membership was back up to 78, and a rare but fine photograph of the opening day at Port Royal was taken by Heath and Bradnee, photographers of Exeter. This picture, outside the public house and on the pontoon, shows around 70 people in attendance. The club purchased its first 'Tub Pair' named *Patience* from Salter Bros. Of Oxford, for £21. Of all the boatbuilders used by the club, Salters is the only one still in existence. It seems that many members had wanted to have a tub pair for several years; another was bought from Salters a few years later, for the same price.

Photo 4: 1903 Opening Day, Port Royal

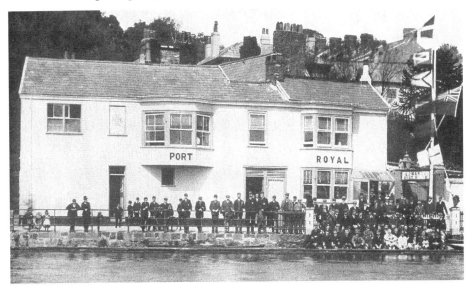

The resurgence of the club at this time seems to have been due

Photo 5: Excester 1912

partly to the arrival of the tub pair, and partly to the influence of one or two key people, notable a Mr. W.S. Goff, who was the leader of this new group. Dart claims that, *'all who came beneath his rule as captain felt the force of his strong personality and his power of keeping men interested and together'*. There was also some good coaching at this time, thanks to Lieutenants Thomson and Benson of the Royal Artillery as well as two clergymen, revs. Mackworth-Drake and Evers, four men who gave generously of their valuable time. We are lucky at present to have highly committed and skilled coaches who are equally willing to give their time and we are seeing the results of this in the clubs performances.

Raising funds was a constant issue for the club as new boats were always needed. In 1904, a Mr. Gidley offered to contribute to the cost of a new four; the club raised £20, and Mr. Gidley made this up to the purchase price of £37. This new four was named *'Minnehaha'*.

Membership by this time, with no entrance fee, was back up to 99, its largest ever up to then. Even the city council was supportive, providing a trolley and rails at the Double Locks to facilitate moving boats across the lock. In 1905, the club won prizes totalling £20 10s at regattas in Totnes, Torquay and Dartmouth; and the Exeter juniors won the WEARA junior championship in 1908. Meanwhile, club members were issued with 'collection cards' so that they could make extra efforts to raise

Photo 6: Club Open Day 1913

prosperity. There had been 550 members since the club began; 24 chairmen, 13 hon. Secretaries and 8 hon. Treasurers. Amazingly, the club had had the same landlord and boatman at the Port Royal, Mr. Charles Edwards, since its formation in 1864. Following on the Club Photo Book, a Celebration Souvenir Book was produced in 1913, 200 copies being printed at a cost of £2 5s 2d, each copy selling for 2s 2d (about 11p). A celebration dinner was planned for the club's 50th anniversary, and an enlargement of a photo of the club's original boat, *St John of Malta,* taken at Double Locks in 1864, was framed and presented to Mr. W.E. Hannaford. Rowing and swimming matches were also planned for July, as was a 'Ladies Day'.

But things were about to change, though perhaps members did not realise this. In August 1914, on the outbreak of war, many members of the club were mobilised and enlisted, including all four members of the successful junior four, who joined the 4th Devon Regiment; regattas were cancelled, and rowing diminished for several years.

THE NEXT 50 YEARS, 1914-1964

In 1912, when the two existing histories of the club come to an end, the ERC Committee consisted of seven men: J.R. Goff, R.H.Dymond, F. Beer, H.S.Beale, H.H.Harding, F. James and W.H. Clements. We know little about these men or their fellow club members at the time; how old were they? What was their background, what work did they do, were they professional men with money to spend on their leisure activities? The only evidence is from Mr. Dart's book which ends with a photo of the entire club on Opening Day at the Turf in 1912, in which there are about 100 people, some in rowing gear, some in club blazers, others in working clothes with hats or caps.

Photo 1: 1912 Opening Day

From the photo, it seems that there was quite a mix of professional people, working boatmen and younger lads. The club's newest boat, the coxed four *Excester*, their first ever centre-seated boat at 36 ft long, was the pride of the club, as can be seen from the wonderful photo of the boat leaving Port Royal included in chapter 2 as photo 5, with a gathering of blazered club members on the pontoon to see them off. The launch was followed by a 'canoe steeplechase' and gig and punt races, both of which caused much amusement. And (unlike today), the festivities ended with the entire club singing 'God Save the King'.

The club seemed to be thriving, not only because of its strong

23

membership but also through the competitive and social events that took place. For example, in 1913, the Blanchford Cup was first awarded for the winner of an open handicap sculling race. Mr Blanchford, presenting the Blanchford Cup and the Vulcan Goblets to the winners, said it gave him great pleasure *'to do anything which would tend to the development of amateur rowing'*.

And the club began to hold swimming matches, under the auspices of the Head Weir Swimming Club, for which prizes were given by various members. It seems slightly worrying from a twenty-first century perspective, that these matches would have been held in the river, which only a year previously had been described in the press as *'nothing more than a series of cess pools'*. Maybe people had a greater resistance to infections in those days! The minutes however show that all these competitive events, and the Ladies' Day, were proving to be very popular. So much so that the committee decided that *'Honorary Members shall only be allowed to use the dinghies once every 14 days'*; clearly pressure on the available boats.

There was also a day on Dartmoor in 1913, after which, it was resolved that winter fixtures should be held, and that the club should introduce a billiards handicap, married and singles whist and skittles competitions, and a *'tripe supper and smoking concert'*. Tripe and smoking would put off lots of people these days, but they must have been popular then, as smoking concerts became a regular feature of the social calendar. Yet the attitudes towards what was appropriate behaviour within the club was indicated by an item in the minutes from July 1914, which resolves that:

> *'the attention of the Captain be drawn to Juniors being on the canal in a racing boat and in racing uniform on Sunday, and that he be asked not to encourage this kind of thing in any way, as the Committee did not think it desirable'*.

The club was clearly active, and had active junior members. All the more sad, therefore, that this thriving club had to be decimated by the impact of the war. In August 1914, the committee minutes show that *'Owing to mobilisation of members of the crew and cancellation of regattas owing to the war, rowing for the season was at an end'*. The Captain reported that all four members of the junior four had joined the 4th Devon Regiment, and the committee resolved that the names of club members who had joined HM Forces should be sent to the *Devon and Exeter Gazette* with a subscription of £2.2s to the Devon Patriotic Fund, from club funds. The list of names

War Memorial of Exeter Amateur Rowing Club

Exeter Amateur Rowing Club hold their annual meeting on Thursday, and the principal feature of the proceedings will be the unveiling of a "Roll of Honour and Photo Memorial," presented to the club by fellow members in London of those who have served with the Colours, and of those who have died for their country. The annual report, to be presented, congratulates the club on being in possession of funds and an organisation in working order to pick up the strings where they had to be dropped in 1914. This result was due to the loyalty of old members in paying their subscriptions, and to Mr. Chas. Edwards, who for several years had presented his account with a very substantial rebate. Mr. S. C. Pyne consented to act as secretary for Mr. E. G. Way since the latter joined the Colours, and one of the results of his energy was the Roll of Honour and Photo Memorial of members with the Army and Navy, which would form a very handsome and lasting memorial of the services of E.A.R.C. men. The membership at the end of the year was as follows: Life members, 5; active, 78 (of whom 40 have ten years' membership); honorary, 7; total, 90.

28th January 1919 article

amounted to a loss to the club of 21 active members. The later minutes of the club do not, however, tell us how many of these returned safely. The only other reference to those members who served in the war is a newspaper article of 1919 which reports the presentation of a photo memorial to the club.

Inevitably, the question of continuing the club during the war was raised and discussed. The Committee however felt that there was no reason for discontinuing the Club, and this was to be brought up at the next AGM.

The St. Thomas Rowing Club was not so lucky. In October 1914, ERC received a letter from them saying that the boats and properties of the club were for sale. It was resolved that the ERC committee visit the St. Thomas boathouse and inspect these boats; but following the visit, the committee was unable to make a recommendation to the general meeting *'owing to the present serious crisis and having regard to the financial state of the club'* and it was resolved not to purchase any of the St. Thomas boats. This was probably wise, as the treasurer's report for the following year showed that the club's balance owed to the treasure was a mere £11, and it was resolved that no dinner be held that year. The St. Thomas Rowing Club was finally dissolved in 1921.

The club may not have been discontinued during the war, and yet there are few records of club activities during the following war years. It is not until 1920 that we have further records of club activity. Rowing seems to have revived, as the minutes show that the club purchased ten pairs of paddles that year, and a further four pairs the following year. Then in 1922, the club bought a new gig and a four-oared gig with oars from Sims and sons of Putney, for a total of £92 13s 6d, named *'City of Exeter'*. Clearly, rowing was back in business. The four *'City of Exeter'* raced from Port Royal to Exe Bridge in 7 mins 28 sec. It was not until 1964 that the senior 'A' crew lowered this record from Exe Bridge to Port Royal to 3mins 24.5 secs! This course now became the agreed Exeter Regatta course.

In 1924, it appears that there was a sale of boats and equipment at the Port Royal. At this sale, the club spent over £17 on the following list of equipment:

One double skiff	£5 15s
One single skiff	£4
One single outrigged skiff	£2 5s
One double outrigged skiff	£3 5s
Three pairs of 10ft paddles	£2 5s

Three pairs of 9ft paddles   £2 17s

In the following year, there was a further outlay of £53 for four second-hand skiffs and four paired sculls, from Mr. H.E. Bartram. There must have been new funds coming into the club for these expenses, but the records give us no indication of their source; was this membership fees, sponsors, or what?

What we do know is that in 1927, the Port Royal Amateur Rowing Club was founded. Our records do not show who the original members were; had they defected from the Exeter club, or were they a completely new set of rowers? It seems that this was probably a breakaway group, as ERC minutes indicate that in 1929, just two years later, Exeter Rowing Club *'finally left the Port Royal';* and the word 'finally' here might suggest that there had been some sort of friction or rift between the old and new clubs that provoked this split. Club activity continued however, albeit at a rather low level. It was agreed that a President and Vice President be elected annually; a cheque for £2 had been received from the Torquay Regatta Committee towards the cost of carriage of boats; and that the finals of the Vulcan Goblets were again held in 1928. In that year, the Captain reported that he had arranged to have the three best dinghies *'scraped and varnished and put in good working order'* together with one of the tub pairs, and that the cost of this , including storage, would be £12. The other tub pairs were also in need of a great deal of repair, but a Mr. Gregory had agreed to do a thorough overhaul for £4.

The club sold off some boats at this time, presumably to cover the costs, including single and double outrigged boats and a small dinghy, cracked and not worth repairing. They also sold off half a dozen pairs of oars, *'as the club could easily spare them'.* It does sound, from these records, that the club was substantially slimmed down since the formation of the Port Royal club. But they continued to exist in parallel; in 1929 for example, the records show that Fred Lee, the brother of the well-known Edgar Lee after whom a club boat is named, was a member of the Port Royal club and rowed in the WEARA junior championship crew. Edgar became a member of the Port Royal Junior Championship crew two years later.

1929 was also the year in which the National Amateur Rowing Association was formed. The rules and constitution of the new Association, which was to control rowing, were discussed and affiliation agreed. The club decided to spend about £3 on *'extending the shelter at Exe Bridge'*, making a small dressing room for members. And a member from the 1930s, a Mr. John Lisle of Cardiff, recollects that there was indeed a

Photo 2: The club at Exe Bridge

'club headquarters' at the Exe Bridge.

Funds were clearly low at this point. The committee decided in 1929 that it *'could not see its way clear to suggest any draw for the annual refund'*. Yet later that year, it was pointed out that the newest of the club's racing fours, the *City of Exeter,* had been purchased seven years earlier, and that all of the other craft were older than this. A Mr. Dorothy had said he was willing to overhaul the two racing fours at the smallest cost possible, around £3, to include *'two coats of varnish and fresh oiled silk'.* The club accepted his kind offer.

It was considered 'imperative', therefore, that the club should raise money for a new boat. However, this did not happen until 1930-31. In the meantime, the club wobbled on, organising a 'Derby Draw in aid of the Boat Fund' in 1930, and inviting local businesses to contribute with prizes. 600 books of tickets were printed and sold. The draw turned out to be a great success, raising over £41 for the New Boat Fund. The club also decided to move its headquarters to the Seven Stars Hotel.

And things seemed to be on the up again. For the first time in years, ERC secured its first win at the Exeter Regatta, with the brothers S.L. and R.W. Pyne winning the Orchard Challenge Cup for Junior Pairs. The brothers had asked to row in the pairs at Dartmouth without also rowing in the fours, but it was decided that unless they competed in the fours, the brothers would not be allowed to enter the pairs race.

The decision was also taken in this year to purchase new boats, and in 1931 an order was placed with Messrs. Sims of Putney for a new four, to be christened *Exon.* In fact, when the new boat was delivered in 1932, it was named the *Exeter.* But the key decision in 1931 concerned the raising of funds for a new boathouse. It was estimated at the time that this would cost around £500, of which £350 would be for labour costs.

But then everything goes very quiet; only a very few club records

Port Royal Rowing Club   Circa   1930
Unknown, Bill Ball, Fred Lee, George Neal, Stan Neal, Charlie Green, F.Dorothy, B.Langmaid, G.Densham,
C.Dorothy, Evenmi, Fisher, G.Williams, W.Jordan, E.Peckam, Edgar Lee.
Coxwains; M.Evenmi, G.Gidley, M.O'Neil, Unknown.

Photo 3: Port Royal Rowing Club Open Day at Turf Locks

exist for the subsequent period up to and including the Second World War (WW2). What is perhaps significant is that the Wall Street Crash of 1929 in the USA had spread to Britain by 1930, followed by years of depression, which reached their peak in 1932. The economic recession, which brought about general strikes and great hardship, was most severely felt in the industrial areas of the midlands and the north; but inevitably it affected all parts of the country, including Exeter. Unemployment nationally rose to around 3.5 million, exports halved, public sector wages were cut drastically, and the Labour government of the time, only the second labour government ever, found itself under huge pressure from trade unions. All this seems a familiar scenario in 2014; yet conditions for the unemployed and business were much worse in the 1930s, as unemployment benefit and social security were limited or non-existent. So it is highly likely that people had little or nothing to spare to fund leisure activities such as rowing.

Nevertheless, the new boat was delivered in July 1932, which with oars cost the club over £95. The next records of the club are from 1938, when members of the two rowing clubs, Port Royal and Exeter, 'rowed in cap and gown' on a course from Port Royal to Exe Bridge one August Saturday afternoon, and were given race medals by the Gaumont Palace after the showing of the film 'A Yank at Oxford' at the cinema. The race and the following celebration seem to have been a popular success.

War intervened again. Virtually all members of the club were now serving in the forces in one form or another, according to J.M. Hodges, the Chairman of the club at the time. In response to a letter in the press, he wrote as follows:

Sir,

> *Exonian's letter of Friday mentions the riverside being made hideous by tumbledown buildings. I must agree, and at the same time confess that the boathouse of the Exeter Amateur Rowing Club by Exe bridge is one of the chief offenders to the eye, becoming more apparent since the removal of the overgrowth surrounding it, revealing the damage caused during the blitz on our city.*

> *95% of the EARC members are now serving in the forces, so no temporary repairs could be made, and, in all conscience, the builders could not be called in when their services are in demand for the blitz repairs.*

> *However, the site demands a more imposing structure and it is my ambition to see a clubhouse constructed worthy of the city of Exeter and worthy of the EARC, remembering that it is one of the oldest established sporting clubs in the country (1864).*

> *All this we hope for when they come back from over there. But, alas it is left to the sportsmen of the city, as finance is the only stumbling block.*

Things seemed to move quickly after this. The new clubhouse was built, Mr. S. Ball taking down a boathouse he had at Exe Bridge and arranging with Mr. Thomas for the loan of a flat barge to bring timber and roofing material to the Port Royal.

And in 1946, the two rowing clubs, Exeter and Port Royal, amalgamated to form a single club. The press announced this as follows:

> *'The new city rowing club, putting its new house in order, as it were, has been giving attention to all available craft idle during the war years. First step was to make both tub pairs fit for training. "Isca" is ready for the river. "Enterprise" is in the last stages of titivation, while one of*

Photo 4: Men's eight crew for the London Head 1949

the racing fours is now receiving attention.'

The records also indicate that, in September 1946:

> *As a preliminary canter to a possible full-scale Exeter Regatta next year, the newly founded Exeter Rowing Club are tomorrow staging a club regatta on the Exe, the course for main events being from Bonhay Weir to the Port Royal, and for lesser events from the ferry to the Port Royal.*

St. Luke's College had proposed that about 40 students attend for training using the Club's tubs and it was agreed that the facilities of the Club be placed at the disposal of St. Luke's College during the winter. A year later, the newly-re-founded club accepted the application of St. Luke's College and the Exeter University boat clubs to join ERC with a minimum subscription of ten shillings (50p) for each member.

In 1947, the club rowed in the Tideway event for the first time.

Then in 1949, the first new boat for many years was purchased, a four christened *Port of Exeter*. Pat Smart, Harry Godbeer, Jack Oaks and Geoff Rice rowed the new boat at Bideford that year in an NARC event, and won the Junior Fours championship of all England.

The club seemed to be thriving again. In 1950, the club entered the Head of the River (Thames) again: Quintin club had agreed to loan a boat, and the crew to travel to London on the 7.30 a.m. train. The subsequent result was an improvement on the previous year's time.

It was agreed that the Exeter colleges should use boats as follows:

University College of the South West: *'Port Royal'* and *'Amelia'*

St. Luke's college: *'Exeter'* and *Exon'*

But the key incident at this time happened in 1950, when ERC, at their recent meeting at Port Royal agreed to recognise the recently formed ladies club. A fund had already been started for a new boat, for the ladies to row in. A 'wardrobe' was acquired the following year; not for the ladies' clothing, though, but for the various cups that had been awarded or won over the years!

1952 saw the official opening of the new boat house at Port Royal by Geoffrey Pring, director of Messrs. Norman and Pring. A bronze plaque of the club badge was unveiled and a silver oar presented to Geoffrey as a memento. A ladies four took to the water and preparations were made for an opening day run to Turf.

1953 saw the coronation of Queen Elizabeth, and to commemorate this, a new boat had been commissioned. It was christened, not surprisingly, *'Queen Elizabeth II'* by Mrs. Beer; but this boat seems not to have been well built.

Crews were complaining that the 'Elizabeth II' was too light a craft for their weight and it appeared the boat was made of porous wood! Photographs showing the corrugation to the skin were sent to Mr G. Sims, the boatbuilder responsible. A scraping was taken and damp cloths applied; it was clear that the wood had swollen. It was suggested that linseed oil be applied to prevent buckling when drying out. The boat continued to be accident prone, as described below. Nevertheless, a new fine four was ordered two years later, from the same makers, and a deposit of £52 paid.

A new cup, the Harry Ehren cup, was presented to the club, to be awarded each year as an annual Challenge Cup for new members who have made most progress during their first year. This award has continued until today. Floods in the river, a feature of the 2012 season when our regatta had to be cancelled twice, are not a new thing. In 1956, the *'Enterprise'* was swept away during an unusually high water, and could not be recovered until the flood subsided.

In April 1955, the current ERC captain visited Mr. Badcoe, headmaster of Episcopal school, *' to obtain several potential new coxes'*. During the visit, Mr. Badcoe said he would like to place rowing on the curriculum and enquired as to what help Exeter Rowing Club could give in this direction. At a later meeting between Mr. Badcoe and club representatives, the following points were drawn up:

1   The school club should have 10 members only

2   The Minimum age should be 14 yrs (excepting coxes)

3   Rowing would take place from 3pm-4.15pm

4   The Sports master to be in charge

5   Each boy should be able to swim 25 yards

In June, approval was given by the education authority for rowing by the pupils of the Episcopal School and training commenced.

The new fine four was ready for collection in February 1956. A new type of blade with hardwood backs was ordered for this boat. Mrs Swain christened it, as she had been instrumental in the commencing of the boat fund. The Christening took place on 13th Sept 1956, and the boat was named "Walter Dorothy", *'in recognition of immense and invaluable contributions this member had made to the club'.*

Boats were now being bought regularly, but others were being sold. The *Exeter,* for example, by this time 20 years old, was sold to RAF St. Eval in Cornwall for £30, while a new tub and fine pair were ordered from Holman's of Exmouth.

A Mr. Bill Gorfin was instrumental in promoting the idea of the 'Head of the Exe' race in 1957 and with other leading Exmothians, donated a silver *"Exmouth Townsman's Trophy"* for the race. The first race was held on 25th May, 1957, the course being from the Port Royal, via Double Locks and Topsham Locks to the Exmouth Coastguard station (some 14 miles). The winners of the trophy were the Exeter University crew. Following the success of this event, the committee agreed that two boats be taken to Exmouth for the purpose of giving crews experience of sea rowing; and in August, It was planned to transport 5 boats to Exmouth for sea rowing, including for the ladies. Later that year, at a commemoration dinner at the Countess Wear Hotel, Marcus Hodges was presented with a silver tankard to mark his 21 years as chairman of the local club. It was kept as a complete surprise to Mr Hodges that he was to be awarded this silver tankard.

There is then a lull in the records for about seven years. One new boat was purchased in 1960, and christened '*Ernest Marks*' in 1962; one boat, the *'Port Royal II'* was also sold in 1962, but there is little other news of the club in those years. A significant event for the club, however, was the great floods of October and December 1960, which inundated most of West Exe from Exwick down to what is now Marsh Barton. It was this event that ultimately led to the building of the current flood channels, and the barrage and sluices above Trew's Weir, opposite the Port Royal.

However, 1964 saw the centenary of the club, and this was not only marked by celebrations, but also seemed to inject new vigour into the club, as the next chapter describes.

THE LAST 50 YEARS, 1964-2014

1964 was the club's centenary year: There was a presentation in July to Ernie and Win Searle of an inscribed tray and set of crystal glasses on occasion of their retirement as host and hostess of The Port Royal Club Headquarters, a token of appreciation from ERC. August saw the new hosts George and Paddy Blundell-Pound welcomed to club headquarters The Port Royal. And during the regatta that year, a young man called Wilf Denning (bow in junior fours) dived into the Exe to save a man in trouble.

In August, the Exeter Regatta was held with 2 senior Exeter crews winning 1st and 2nd in the senior 4s race and making club history and establishing a club record in the process. Chairman (Marcus Hodges) observed *"never before in the history of the club has this happened and the club is justly proud of its senior crews"*.

1964 also saw the first edition of the ERC Newsletter, which reported the inaugural Swan's Nest Cross Country Run and the Annual Dinner in April, but sadly, the year did not end well. The coxed four *Elizabeth II*, which had already proved an unlucky boat, was again involved in an accident, described in the press as follows:

Winning Boat Cut In Half

A crowd of 5000 gasped as a 36ft long coxed racing four lost control in the grip of a fast growing tide and was swept helpless among moored craft of Shaldon.

The boat, "Elizabeth II" belonging to the ERC overturned, throwing its crew of five into the swirling water. Broadside it continued, crashing in to a second moored vessel, which cut it in two.

The sleek polished hull of the racing craft was shattered into matchwood.

Rescue craft quickly left the shore. At first it was feared a member of the crew was missing. Only four could be seen clinging to the shattered hull as it was carried upstream on the tide.

The fifth member managed to grab a mooring chain and clung to the side of a boat until picked up.

As the splintered remains of the Exeter boat were brought ashore, almost spontaneously a collection was started for the club, which resulted in £47 towards a new boat estimated to cost £350.

Photo 1: New flag ceremony

Being the centenary year, the local press held many articles about the club's history, which were collected together in a large Scrapbook. The articles and photos document the many successes of the club over the years, listing championships won, the launching of new boats and various celebratory events, including a centenary dinner at the Imperial Hotel, and mayoral receptions in the guildhall. The press also pointed out the growing links with 'rowing nurseries' in some of the local schools, including Episcopal, Hele's and Bishop Blackall.

The following year saw a New Flag ceremony at Port Royal, to mark the close of a century of rowing history. The new flag, subscribed for by the Vice Presidents, was presented to the President, M. C. B. Hoare, by Marcus Hodges, senior Vice President. After the President acknowledged receipt, the flag was hoisted by John Ibbett. Later that year, the Junior 4 were the WEARA Champions and the Senior A 4 were runners up in their category. And on Boxing Day, a new landing stage, presented by Pat Smart, was towed from the Quay to the Port Royal. The year also saw the launching of the *Marcus Hodges,* described as 'the club's most successful boat ever'.

In autumn 1960, Exeter had been hit by the worst flooding in years, affecting St. Thomas, Exwick and Alphington very badly. It was clear that some kind of flood prevention would have to be undertaken; and in 1965 this work began. as the construction of the sluices and flood channel opposite Port Royal had now begun, the regatta races had again to be run from Exe Bridge to Port Royal. A new rule was also introduced whereby all coxswains would wear life jackets when afloat. The big plus for rowers that year, though, was the installation of hot showers in the men's and ladies' dressing rooms, an amenity long awaited. A nominal sum of 3d (1p!) was expected to be paid by all who availed themselves, and a box was supplied for this purpose.

In 1966, the Newsletter shows that the regatta draw made a profit for the Club, and that there were now more young members in the Club as well as more crews taking an active part in competition. Even so, the Treasurer reported that for the fourth year running, the Club had shown a loss which was nearly all due to rising costs. However, gas and water bills were fully covered by the shower fund. Fortunately, **another** Trust Fund Gift was received, to provide new boats. ERC could now look forward to a new boat every two or three years, it was said, thanks to the generosity of one of its keenest vice presidents Mr Geoffrey Pring. David Macklin also reported that he had been able to obtain a grant from the Education Committee for 50% of the cost of a new boat. A further significant event in July of that year was ERC rowing at Henley Royal Regatta for the first time, in the coxless 4s Wyfold Trophy event. However, there were always new battles to be fought; and during the year, a campaign had to be fought to keep the Exeter Canal open for leisure and rowing.

New trophies also came to the club this year. A silver salver presented by H. S. Northcote, M.P. to the Regatta Committee in 1883 was handed over to ERC. And a silver miniature trophy, presented to ERC for some competitive purpose, was one of four presented to the Senior 4 Championship crew of 1907/08/09 who won the J. H. Lile cup (now in the Guildhall) outright at Bideford. A miniature trophy was presented by S. K. Bates and is inscribed "Alfred Dorothy, St. Thomas ARC". A second silver miniature trophy has also been presented to the Club by Ernest Marks and is inscribed "Alfred Marks". The Ernest Marks Perpetual Exeter Regatta Trophy for 4 oared police crew was presented to HQ Division 1966 Police Champions.

In February 1967, a new racing four named *"James Smeall"*, built by Edwin Phelps, was christened at Port Royal for St. Luke's Boat Club. The St. Luke's Boat Club was celebrating its 21st anniversary. And the new eight, *John Percival,* was housed at Countess Wear by courtesy of the University Boat Club for practice on the canal on Sunday mornings. This year also saw the 11th rowing of the Head of the Exe race. The newsletter also reported a curious piece of news, as follows:

> *"It was on Sunday that four young ladies in a boat with coxen, that is before the ferry wire claimed coxen Mike Wills, suspended high and wet, whilst the ladies 'gone with the wind' downstream!!!"*

The year also saw the launch of a new boat for the ladies section, christened *Queen of the Exe*. And the press reported excitedly that the first ever eights races had been held during the Totnes regatta, attracting large crowds of onlookers.

In February 1968, the boat house again flooded in the recent Exe rising and Valentine's Day was given over to cleaning up! April saw the 15th head of the river race for scullers under A.R.A. rules, from Mortlake to Putney, 4 ½ miles (the reverse of the current Oxford and Cambridge course). Dave Macklin, Pat Smart and Russell Andrews took part. This was the first ever club entry in this event.

David came 171st, in 23mins 57; Russell 262nd, in 25mins21, and Pat 327th, in 28mins04. The overall winner's time was 21mins28!

The year also saw both ladies and men's sections receiving an influx of newcomers. Two members, named only as Russell and Wilf, went to Mexico to support the GB squad in the rowing events. And there was what now seems like perennial concern expressed about the way the sculls were being treated and a resolution was passed: *"No novice oarsman shall use the fine sculls until he has satisfied either the Captain or the Vice Captain that his ability to use them meets the required standard."*

The good news was that the treasurer reported that for the first time in 4 years, the Club had shown a surplus of income over expenditure of £26.15.7. The 1967 dinner made a profit of £4.11s 11d, helping to reduce the loss made on the 1966 dinner, and the Ladies jumble sale raised £4. 1s 3d.

In 1969, there was an incident involving the landing stage that had come adrift and was discovered down stream, *'Knocking' at the grill of The Paper Mill Water Race'*. A rescue crew took to the water and with help from the bank, towed it to safety, narrowly missing the weir with its swift flow. At the AGM, however, the treasurer again reported a loss of £85.11.5; Club finances were at their lowest since 1950. The new set of blades cost £113.0.6. Expenses had included the boat trailer overhaul at a cost of £48.8.0., new set of oars £48, repairs to old oars £21, four sculling boats at a cost of £550.15.0. Despite the financial problems in the club, ERC finished 1st, 2nd and 3rd in the Head of the Exe race.

1970 was the next eventful year for the club. For only the second time in their history, ERC Senior Four became Champions of the West. The new Exe Bridge was now in the course of being constructed and would not be complete until June or July of 1972. It was therefore decided that the City's regatta would take place on a much shortened course (Port Royal to ferry wire) and because of this, no championship points would be awarded in the rowing events. Although the shortened course forced on the organisers of the Exeter regatta proved popular with both competitors and spectators, it was believed at the time that *'there is no possibility of it becoming a permanent feature of future regattas, because it would not measure up to West of England Championship requirements'*. It is interesting therefore that we are still rowing our regatta over this shortened course today.

The women's section of ERC held their 21st birthday celebrations at Wingfield Park Social Centre, Heavitree, in 1971. Former chairman Mrs R. Moore cut the cake watched by the first crew members of 1950.

But membership must have been down, as in April, "Join the Rowing Club" car stickers for ERC were now in circulation, as part of a drive to recruit new members. The club had a full page write up in the

Photo 2: 1974 Police Champions

Express & Echo on this day, sponsored by local business interests, as well as a pictorial display in the window of the Cheltenham and Gloucester Building Society in Paris Street, which showed rowing items of interest and details of an Open Club Night at the Port Royal, with the invitation to meet the Captain and members and inspect the equipment. Nevertheless, it turned out to be quite a successful year, as ERC won the first Head of the Dart, and completed the double by winning the Head of the Exe on May 22nd. The Secretary had received a letter from Messrs. Daw & Son informing the Club of a legacy of £250 left to the Club by the late A. C. D. Pain, and the Treasurer reported a surplus again. But at the AGM, the President expressed an urgent need for new club and boathouse premises.

In 1972, the regatta committee decided they would like the races to be staged over the shortened course again with full West of England Championship points being awarded to the crews. And *"The Committee agreed to pay the cost of 2p per mile for taking boats to regattas."* This may have been an incentive, as In 1972 ERC won the Heads of the Exe, Dart and Plym. The Police Constabulary requested facilities for their cadets to row, using only the tub, and the Committee agreed to this request at a charge of £1 per person.

Photo 3: 1970 Club Photo

ERC also competed in the Boston Marathon (i.e. Boston Lincolnshire, not Massachusetts!) for the first time in 1972, finishing second to Henley Rowing Club in the 4s event. Clearly the club was doing very well in competitions at this time; and the year marked the inauguration of *a* practice row for the newly-formed Vets VIII crew in "*Shadowfax*". A big breakthrough for the older end of the club.

In 1970, a Club photo had been taken for the first time since 1959.

A recruitment drive also seems to have been quite successful, attracting about 8 new members. There were adverts in the local press, including one headed, *ENJOY ROWING- JOIN NOW* which went on to invite 15-20 year-olds to come and '*learn about the great game of rowing*' and to '*experience the thrill and art of oarsmanship*'. But the Port Royal launching pontoon was said to be in a sorry state due to the ravages of winter flood water, and needed repair or replacement. Luckily, a letter and cheque for £20 was received from Whitbread Devon Ltd. (presumably the brewers who owned the Port Royal?) towards the cost of repairing the fixed raft.

On the 4th of July, therefore, '*Operation Landing Stage*' began at 6.30 a.m.! Nick Parkin, the 'Architect in Chief', reported that to repair the fixed raft would require 6 hours' work with welding and cutting plant on site and he would require two further helpers. Help was provided by club members, particularly Frank Lewis, Pat Smart, Owen Burridge and new member Steve Ash. Steel frame welded and drilled, took shape, then fitting of elm planks took place on the second day. Harry Branton arranged delivery of planks, thanks to the brewery for their monetary contribution. The Committee was informed that H. Branton P would pay the difference between the Whitbread cheque and the total cost of the wood for the raft.

In early 1972, Exeter University Boat Club informed ERC that a new boat house would shortly be built adjoining the existing one, with changing rooms and showers. A letter from N. Bull of Exeter University Boat Club offered to meet representatives of ERC to discuss new premises, and it was decided to form a joint sub-committee. By March, M. Baker said that a meeting between the Club and Exeter University resulted in a good many ideas passing between both clubs *'regarding the possibility of a dual development at the Swing Bridge'*. A further meeting was to be arranged, and it was hoped that a meeting with the Town Clerk would clarify certain plans.

In 1973, an event took place at Stithians Reservoir in Cornwall, advertised as *'something new for Cornwall'*. It turned out to be a contest between Falmouth and Exeter rowing clubs, and was advertised as the first *'sliding seat skiff rowing'* in Cornwall. The publicity also invited responses to two questions; *'Is it possible to hold a full scale regatta at Stithians?'* And, *'Could this become the Henley of the South West?'!*

Fund raising became prominent again in 1974 with the inauguration of the '100 Club'. The publicity for this was widespread, as follows:

> *"We at Exeter Rowing Club look upon this as an extra effort to raise enough money to build our own Clubhouse. Over many years we have wanted to provide ourselves with a Clubhouse both as a Social Centre for Members and their Supporters, and as a Water Sports Centre.*
>
> *Rowing is an expensive amateur sport and our energies in recent years have been directed at purchasing first class equipment whilst maintaining membership fees at an acceptable level.*
>
> *In asking you to support us, either by means of a Bankers Standing Order for £1.50 per quarter, or an annual subscription of £6.00, we hope that you will be able to identify with our efforts. Your subscription will qualify you for inclusion in our monthly draw known as the Regatta Draw of which two "Grand Slam" draws will have an extra large prize. One in Mid-Summer will be the Henley Draw and the other in Mid-Winter will be our Christmas Draw."*

In 1974, the AGM reported that the year ended with the Club "in the black". M. Baker had provided the Club with a new set of blades and had asked that they be for the use of the young crew members. He was thanked for this valuable addition to Club equipment.

1975 turned out to be a key year for women in the club, as it saw the merger of men's section and ladies section, the ladies becoming full members of ERC. And only a year later, the women members celebrated by winning the Open Ladies event at the annual South Coast Regatta. The Junior crew were also champions at the same regatta. During the year, records show that the Club had rowed in 10 head races, 19 regattas and the Boston Marathon, which involved crews in a total of almost 150 separate races. Exeter finished third in the National 1975 Regatta tables, behind Hereford and Derby, an improvement of one place from the 1974 results. A display of trophies had been arranged at the Britannia Building Society.

Also in 1975, Miss Mabel Carter, a former Exeter resident, wanted to find a suitable resting place for two family heirlooms. Miss Carter had been left two rowing medals belonging to her father, Mr Alfred Orchard Carter who used to row on the Exe back in the days when the ERC was first formed. One of the medals, a Maltese Cross, had been presented in

Photo 4: Return visit to Rennes

1864, the year of the rowing club's inception; the other medal was a tiny gold rowing boat which had *'Exeter regatta 1874'* inscribed on it. Mr Len Rey, custodian of the archives at ERC, said he would be delighted to accept the medals on behalf of the club.

A grant to the Club of £366 had been made by the Devon Playing Fields Association. The issue was raised of the high cost for individuals rowing at the South Coast Championships in Shanklin. It was agreed that the Club would help with a sum of £20, and £15 expenses would come from WEARA, in addition to generous donations from N. Parkin and J. Ibbett. A rota was arranged for overhauling Club equipment during the winter.

In 1976, a fund-raising row on the river was made special by the presence of stars from the popular TV period drama series, *The Onedin Line,* much of which had been filmed on Exeter Quay. The sponsored rowers, which included Peter Gilmore, the actor who played Captain Onedin, was from the Port Royal to Bonhay Weir by the Mill on the Exe, and participants had to complete the course to earn their sponsorship.

The Club received a grant of £265 from Devon County Council. To help cover the higher expenses incurred attending regattas, it was agreed competing members fees will be increased from 50p to £1. President Edgar Lee donated £100 to the Boat Fund and thanks were expressed for his support.

Tributes were paid to the late Marcus Hodges and members stood in his memory. But perhaps the best tribute was paid by the successes of the club that year, when both Senior A and Senior B crews were WEARA champions, and most rowers in the club were winning in different competitions. They also had their best ever result in the Head of the River that year, with the eight coming 69th and the fours 22nd and 42nd respectively.

Although there had been a visit to the twin city of Rennes in 1962, April 1977 saw ERC make their first return visit to Rennes in Brittany, on the occasion of the Rennes Rowing Club's centenary. More on this link is found in chapter 10. Plans for a Boat House for ERC at Countess Wear were turned down by the planning committee, access from the site onto the by-pass being given as the reason. It was felt that the ERC centre must be based at the Port Royal to attract regular new members and it was agreed that after the London Head some boats would return to Port Royal, thereby creating interest again on the Exe. However, it was agreed that a re-application was to be made for planning permission at Countess Wear now that the Exeter by-pass had been de-trunked with the opening of the M5 motorway.

The council turned down requests for funds as they said there was no money available that year. Replies to requests for sponsorship stated that the various companies were unable to help the Club due to their full commitment on other projects, except Heavitree Brewery who sent £10, explaining that they were unable to do more because of great demand on them this Jubilee Year.

In the following year, a perpetual trophy was donated by Mrs. Ann Hodges in memory of her husband Marcus, to be presented by Mrs. Hodges at Exeter regatta to the 'C' sculls winner, and to be known as the "*Marcus Hodges cup*". In June, a new boat christening took place at Port Royal, attended by the Mayor and Mayoress. The new boat was a carbon craft, 45' long costing £2,300, and was named *"Muriel Toy"*. Later that year, as St. Lukes' College was about to amalgamate with the University and become the School of Education, the St. Lukes and Exeter University boat clubs decided to amalgamate. And later in October, an Open Day was held at Port Royal with the emphasis on recruitment of new members. In November, the Annual Small Boats Head (formerly Head of the Exe) was run from Turf to Countess Wear on the canal.

In 1979 at the WEARA AGM, Len Rey of ERC was invested as President. The club's records also mentioned the sad and recent death of Ernie Searle, former landlord of the Port Royal, who had always shown a great interest in the ERC. But worries were expressed over the funding of Exeter Regatta, partly due to the disappearance of the '*Regatta Fair*' which had sponsored the regatta to the tune of £300. Fortunately, in 1980, the regatta's future was to some extent secured, at least for the time being, by news of a £225 council grant. At the Sports Day at Port Royal that year, the Vulcan Pairs Trophy (donated by L. Pyne and R. Pyne) was presented along with the Miss Ross trophies. The Vulcan Pairs Trophy dates back to 1913 and was originally won by the Pyne brothers in three successive years from 1930-32. And in the same year, ERC competed in the Henley Town & Visitors Regatta, though there are no records of how well they performed.

1979 saw the success of the Senior A crew of Sean McHugh, Dave Manning, Ray Mallett and Dave Pengilley, with cox Geraldine Brown, who lifted the WEARA championship with their win at Dartmouth. In the following year, this crew generously stood down to allow the club's promising youngsters to compete; and the under-16 crew of Chris Cox, Allan Hodgson, Chris Boardman and Paul Vaggers were describes as 'the most promising that the club and the West of England had seen in years', being poised to move up and emulate the successes of their seniors. In 1981 the Senior A crew were back in winning ways though; with Ian Dryden replacing Dave Manning, they picked up where they left off and won the WEARA title again, winning the premier fours event at several of the local regattas, including a big win at Torquay.

There was also drama before the Exeter regatta that year, when on a windy day, Plymouth rowing club's trailer carrying five boats was caught in a freak gust on the A38 and all five boats were damaged, thus unable to row.

1981 turned out to be a crucial year, as planning permission was given for the new ERC HQ at Haven Road. ERC had to vacate Port Royal by 31st December. Offers of temporary accommodation in Haven Road had been made whilst new premises converted, but this was purely for boat storage with no changing or showering facilities. Records have this comment on the momentous change about to happen:

> *On the 31st December, 1981, a 35-year old tradition which this Club held with The Port Royal ended, the club having finally moved out and found itself homeless. The Club is now somewhat fragmented, based partly at premises at the canal basin and at university premises on the canal. Low club moral due to this.*

Social life still centred around The Port Royal, however, and the new owners seemed sympathetic to this. A new launching Raft was

Photo 5: Sean McHugh and Ian Dryden

46

supplied by City Council.

The architect, meanwhile, was working on detailed drawings for new Club House. Club trophies were temporarily displayed at the Prospect Inn, where club members were welcomed by the landlord (Mike Perkins). But despite the prospect of a new clubhouse, active membership of the club was still dwindling and lack of junior members meant that the Club was unable to build new crews. At the same time, the minutes suggest that there was not enough equipment to go round, leading to a new boat and equipment fund being set up, which eventually totalled £226.53 An overall loss of £288 was reported in the minutes, with the brief comment *'Dismal year'*. Members' subscriptions totalled £560.00, rent was £10.00 (£40 in 1980), but there was a profit of £91.00 from the sale of club ties! Perhaps to mitigate some of the funding and membership problems, The Exe Water Sports Association was formed, comprising ERC, Exeter Canoe Club and Exeter Sub-Aqua Club.

In September, ERC cox Andy Jones was presented with an inscribed tankard in appreciation of his service to the club by chairman Paul Wilson, on his departure to Southern Ireland with family. His father Alan Jones, landlord of Double Locks Hotel, was a great supporter of ERC. Double Locks had remained popular with ERC members down through the ages since 1864 and before.

In October 1981, Planning permission having been given by Exeter City Council for new headquarters at 62 Haven Road, the steering committee chaired by Douglas Crosse went ahead with plans to accommodate the three clubs of Exe Water Sports Association. It was hope that the new HQ would be completed within 2 years after the preliminaries of signing council lease and fund raising. The proposed plans for the layout of the new boat house were shown to members by Paul Wilson in December. Clearing of the club house at The Port Royal took place before Christmas, prior to the final move out on New Year's Eve. Boats were transported to a temporary home at 57 Haven Road, complete with ERC sign from Port Royal.

In 1982, a Boat House report at Committee meeting pointed out that the first phase of the erection of 'ablutions' at cost of £20,000 would form the first application for Sports Council grant aid. The other clubs were also working hard to secure financial assistance. The cost of the whole project was estimated at £79,000, *'reducing to £49,000 if labouring and other jobs were done by members'* £160 was paid for preparation of plans for the boat house to be sited at the Swing Bridge, but this plan was shelved. The Princess Alexandra public house on Bonhay Road near the Flowerpot (now no longer in existence) was up for sale and was then thought to be an ideal location for the Club. But nothing came of this.

But there was some good news, as Sean McHugh and Ian Dryden gained a place in the prestigious Henley Royal Regatta. Ian Dryden was also successful in 1986, being selected for the Great Britain squad.

Inevitably, the hiatus led to the club undertaking a great deal of "off the water" training; but this seems to have been a success, as records show more of a younger element in the Club now. Two television programmes highlighted the activities of the club, filming them on the water, one being a TSW film of Ted Tuckerman's visit to the Club in February 1982. The veterans were the most successful crew of the year, with 13 wins and a trip to Amsterdam to take part in F.I.S.A. World Veteran Regatta on October 1st.

Meanwhile, Exe Water Sports Association was going ahead with plans to develop 62 Haven Road, the current site of the boathouses. The Sports Council made available £4,000 as grant aid to start phase 1, and the City Council made available a grant to Exeter Water Sports Association of £950 to pay for the architect to draw up plans for toilet and shower blocks. However, it was thought that these may have to be made available to the public. No bid was put in for Princess Alexandra public house due to "lack of communication": although considered an ideal premises, the pub eventually sold to another party. The Treasurer proposed an increase in membership fees to a minimum of £20 per year for an adult member.

In 1983, ERC Novice Ladies shared with Bideford Reds the WEARA Novice Ladies Championship. Later that year, the builders started work on the foundations in Haven Road. The Annual Report mentions of Boat House development state with some relief that in January, a Sports Council grant of £20,250 had been approved. An interest-free loan from the City Council of £18,000 was also agreed for the conversion of the cottage at 62 Haven Road, to include changing and showering facilities. However, this would be at a rental of £5,000 per year, which was considered too steep. At the time, membership totalled a mere 43 names, plus some honorary Exeter University members as a thank you for the use of their facilities at Countess Wear. The Club had, it claimed, only two raceable craft, but despite this, and the declining support, ERC won 36 trophies during the year!

In February 1984, ERC competed in the New Ross Marathon in Ireland for the first time, winning the Veteran event and also a Waterford glass decanter for the fastest British crew. The New Ross Marathon is a race held annually in February under the auspices of the Irish Amateur

Rowing Union (IARU) and the New Ross club on the river Barrow, over an 18km course from St. Mullins to New Ross.

In May, the first phase of the building work, which had started the previous November, was nearing completion. Great progress had been made on the building to be used as the boat house. And things seemed to be on the up, as the 100 Club made a contribution of £2,000 towards the formation of the Exeter Water Sports Association. The 100 Club scheme, started ten years earlier, had fulfilled the original purpose of the Fund and monthly Draw, i.e. to contribute substantially towards the cost of the new boat house and Club premises.

In June 1984, the minutes report sadly that Ruth Alty died in a rock climbing accident with her boyfriend, Adrian Wadlow from Teignmouth, in the Wye Valley. Ruth joined ERC in 1979 and quickly became a great asset to the Ladies section. Her warmth and dedication, it was reported, would be greatly missed by all who knew her. As a mark of the esteem in which her memory was held, the ERC presented a trophy to be designated "*The Ruth Alty Cup*" for perpetual competition at Exeter regatta. Also that year, Councillor Jack Davis, past president of ERC, suffered a massive heart attack while motoring in Plymouth with his wife Phyllis and collided with a wall. Sadly he never recovered consciousness. Jack was a councillor for St. Leonard's and Deputy Mayor in 1980/81.

Notable successes of the year including the holding of the 120th Exeter Regatta; ERC winning the first Eights race held at Wimbleball; and a Veteran Four competing in the FISA World Veteran Championships in Ghent, Belgium. The ERC Vets were clearly a force to be reckoned with at this time, as in 1985, veterans Sean McHugh and Pete Hogden won the coxless pairs at the National Vets Championship in Loughborough, as well as the coxless pairs race at Thames Head, from Mortlake to Hammersmith. The club members clearly enjoyed going over to Ireland for the New Ross Marathon, as in February 1986, the ERC won "*fastest overseas IV*' title at New Ross Marathon. And a year later, ERC Ladies followed this up by winning their class at the same regatta. ERC Vets Four were the fastest overseas IV and second overall.

1987 also turned out to be a good year for the club. At the Plymouth regatta, in the first event, the veteran's four, Paul Wilson, Ray Mallett, Russell Andrews and Richard Willows, with cox Geraldine Brown, pulled away to win from Bideford Reds to gain a convincing win, despite almost gale force winds and Russell Andrew's seat jamming half way through the race. The Senior B crew of John Walker, Clive Ponsford, Ian Palfrey and club captain Jim Galt, coxed by Tracy Jenkin, also came from behind to beat Bideford Reds. The Senior C fours also turned out to be a dead heat between Exeter and Bradford on Avon. Sadly, the Exeter boat broke its back due to wind and heavy swell after the end of this race.

Photo 6: 1987 Club photo at the new home

1987 also saw Ian Dryden competing at Henley in an attempt to build on his success of previous years, where he had won the Queen Mother's Cup in the quad sculls in 1985 and been a finalist in the Prince Phillip Cup for coxed fours in 1986. The press reported that success at Henley in the Diamond Challenge Cup would enhance his chances of a place in next year's Olympic squad.

In 1988, the local press reported that 'an Exeter rowing family achieved a unique sporting double'. This referred to veteran rower Denzil Hitt, still enjoying a career as one of the top oarsmen of his time in the West of England, and his son Neil. Denzil had won various championships over 25 years or more, since his triumph in the South Coast Championship in 1962 with Brian Sculpher, John Ibbett and Nick Parkin. But now his son had followed in father's footsteps by leading his crew of Andy Hopgood, Steve Midcalf and Steve Aplin, with cox Jane Burrows, to victory once again in the SCC at Bideford.

The same year, ERC seniors, Ladies and vets between them won in five categories at the Plymouth Head of the River. The crews visited

Ireland again for the New Ross Head of the River, when 32 crews participated, including eight from England.

Success continued in 1989. The Dartmouth regatta was rowed on a sweltering hot day, but Exeter once again dominated proceedings with seven victories to take the overall trophy. The best performance came from the Senior C crew of Colin Casselden, Dave King, Paul Fitzhenry and Neil Fitzhenry, coxed by Susie Overall. Despite having to go through two re-rows to qualify for their final, they produced a superhuman effort to storm to victory over Torpoint and Bideford Reds. The Ladies were also very successful, in the Senior B fours as well as in the pairs. The B crew was made up of Helen Clarke, Julia Mockett, Sarah Barker and Clare Connington, coxed by Geraldine Brown; the A crew, which split for the pairs, included Sarah Lighton, Fiona Willmott, Angela Mallett and Helen Treble. These pairs went on to win in both the Senior B and C categories.

The Exeter regatta that year marked 125 years of rowing in Exeter, and the club celebrated by winning no less than ten categories. A big surprise was when the Exeter B crew (Dave Connington, Dave Aplin, Bryan Waycott and Tim Spencer, coxed by Scott Andrews) stormed to a surprise victory over their own A crew. They then joined together for victory in the open eights. The Ladies dominated in the Under-18 categories, as well as in the Senior C class. The crew of Sarah Lighton, Fiona Willmott, Angela Mallett and Nikki Hurved, coxed by Helen Trebble, powered to an amazing double. And to cap the day, the veterans also had a big win over their great rivals, Bideford reds. Neil Hitt, Dave Connington, Michael Mallett and Nikki Hurved all winning in singles. And finally, at the SCC that year, in perfect conditions at Bideford, the Exeter Senior crew that had been so successful at their home regatta shocked their much-fancied rivals BTC Southampton by pulling off their first victory in six years at the SCC.

Earlier in 1989, the club welcomed Tim Crooks to do a coaching session with some of the younger hopefuls. Tim had recently won the Diamond Sculls at Henley, and represented Great Britain at the Montreal Olympics, where he won a silver medal in the men's eight. In 1988 he had defied his veteran status to triumph in the Channel 4 TV Leyland DAF Speed Trials; and in 1989, his absence had made way for Steve Redgrave to take the title. Tim's dominance of the sport covered not only the sprints but also long-distance disciplines; he held the record time for a sculler in the 32-mile Boston Marathon. The local rowers to benefit from his coaching were Neil Hitt and Dave Connington, who had hopes of success at Henley in 1990.

In 1990, Exeter crews competed in the Evesham Regatta over a kilometre course on the Avon. The notable success was Sarah Hopgood, who had an emphatic victory in the Women's Novice sculls. Sarah subsequently got to the semi-final of the open women's sculls at Henley Women's regatta. The women's four (Helen Clarke, Julia Mockett, Sarah Barker and Claire Connington, with cox Rachel Tucker) also came a close second to City of Bristol.

1991 saw the club bring off one of the best coups in its history, when they again engaged the famous Penny Chuter, GB Principal National Coach, to present a coaching seminar on 'New British Training Methodology'. Several coaching visits had been made by Penny in 1974, and these had been enthusiastically attended by Club members.

It was also reported that 'the new boat is almost with us'. This was to be a competitive boat, helped by a generous donation from one of the senior members of the club.

The 1991 regatta, under the new Club Chairman Paul Wilson, was notable for six wins but several disappointments. Success in the fours came from the Ladies senior crew of Erin Taylor, Amelia Christian, Amanda Nash and Julie Souch, coxed by Michael Mallett. Exeter also dominated the sculling races, with Sarah Hopgood and Neil Hitt having fine wins. These two went on to compete in the National Championship that year in Nottingham, where conditions proved to be very difficult. Exeter's women rowers in general had a good year, with three wins at Wimbleball in the open fours, open eights and the Senior novice fours.

On the social side, Annual Dinners continued to attract plenty of club support. In 1995 the members sat down at the Rougemont to a dinner of Pate Maison, Chicken Supreme and Profiteroles, before hearing from the Vice-Chairman about the club's successes over the past year. These included no less than 114 wins at 21 separate regattas, with the Victor Ludorum cup coming to Exeter in nine of these. Quite a season. The Vice Chairman congratulated all the WEARA clubs on the spirit of friendship and cooperation that had existed between all member clubs.

In 1996, WEARA produced a Centenary Handbook, which showed that Exeter had been one of the most successful clubs in the region. Over the 50 years, ERC had been senior champions six times, mostly in the 1970s and 80s. In 1995, ERC had a clean sweep of Senior championships, winning the A, B and C categories, as well as the Ladies Senior C and the Men's novices. The championship Shield for Senior men went to the crew of M. Trevett, J. Smallwood, A. Albutt and T. Ellingham, with K. Simmons coxing. And the Centenary Shield came to ERC also, with a total of 141 wins, almost double that of next best crew, Torquay.

The following year, an ERC pair, Neil Hitt and Peter Hogden, entered the Atlantic Rowing Race. The start of race was in Tenerife on 12th October, finishing in Barbados before Christmas (hopefully, they said!). The boat was launched officially in Dartmouth in May, and the ERC duo started their training on the sea around Dartmouth. In early January 1998, it was announced that Neil Hitt and Peter Hogden came 7th.

The Exeter Canal and the river were frozen solid from the end of December 1997 to mid January 1998, the first time that the Exe had completely frozen since 1982!

1999 proved to be a significant year in that no less than three ERC eights rowed in the head of the river races, an unprecedented event for the club. The first two crews did the Head of the River and the third crew did the Veterans Head of the River on the Sunday.

The crews were as follows:

Neil Hitt, Alasdair Stewart, Greg Anson, Pete Shaw, Don Fraser, Jerry Copping, Rich Eaton, Chris Rogers. Cox: Zoe Flood. 234th out of 401.

Tim Burling, Jon Galt, Mike Robertson, Nick Townsend, George Fuhri-Snethlage, Andy Cook, Andy Marley, Andy Brimblecombe. Cox: Pete Cork. 354th out of 401.

Kevin Dentith, Don Fraser, Paul Wilson, Russell Andrews, Justin Smallwood, Jerry Copping, Greg Anson, Pete Hogden. Cox: Annette Dentith. 41st out of 108.

The following year, 2000, ERC also won the Junior/Senior fours at the SCC in Appledore, the winning crew comprising Michael Robertson, Diccon Haynes, Stephen Power and Jerry Copping, with Peter Cork coxing. In 2001 at Weybridge, Peter Cork won the Novice Sculls and Rachel Painter the WS2 Sculls. ERC also won the Double Sculls Novice class at Upper Thames, and Alasdair Stuart won the Henley Long Distance Sculls. Alasdair continued to do well at Squad Trials, coming back from training camp in Belgium where he came 3rd at U23. The following year at Boston, he came first in the U23 sculls and 6th at lightweight, both outstanding performances.

At Marlow Spring Regatta, ERC were winners at MS3 4+ and WS3 8+. Alasdair Stuart continued to impress in his bid to represent GB: in the final trials in Hazewinkel he showed again that he was the fastest U23 in a scull and the 5th fastest Lightweight overall. He went to Duisburg where he had been selected for the U23 and Lightweight 1x. Later that year, Alasdair reported that he had been offered and had accepted the opportunity to train (as from January) with the Lightweight Squad at Windsor and the Committee offered its congratulations. Kevin Dentith was also highly commended by the ARA for his services to senior rowing.

In 2003, the club sent congratulations to Mel Moore on selection for the GB Squad. Harriet Rawlings was also included in the J18 potential squad with trials in November. Grant money came available for rowers on the fringe of the Squad, which basically helped the likes of Harriet and Mel, with £3m. available over the next two years. A decision was also made about new members, who would be advised to turn up on the first Sunday of each month and meet Paul Wilson. They would receive 10 'learn to row' sessions for £30 and would be required to pay the balance of the subscription after two months. In 2005, Harriet Rawlings was selected for the Junior GB VIII and trained in a pair with a GB candidate from Stratford.

The Committee was informed in 2005 of a £4,000 bequest from Ray Chamberlain's estate, and consideration as to how this should be used was to be given at a future meeting. It was eventually agreed to use the bequest for the new ramp which will be marked with a plaque to commemorate him. EWSA received £5,700 (its annual rent grant) from the City Council. However, the state of changing rooms was deemed unsatisfactory: quotes had to be obtained from cleaning companies. Boat insurance for the year was £2,919.78, ARA affiliation fees £636.50 and rent £2,200.

In 2006, Matt Jacobs and Alice Green were preparing for the GB trials at Boston. The following year, Alice raced at the Bristol Head and broke the course record for WJ18 Single by over 20 seconds. At the Boston Marathon, the men's four were the quickest coxed four of the day, completing the course in 3hrs 55mins. December saw the first of ERC's Winter Head races, which proved to be the biggest event yet, with 199 entries.

From here on, there are many current members of the club with first-hand memories of the last ten years or more, so it seemed appropriate to tell the story of this recent period in their words. The second part of chapter 9 on '*Notable Figures in the Club's History*', therefore, is made up of a series of brief interviews with key people who have served the club well and selflessly over this period. Inevitably, in a club of over 150 members, not everyone of significance could be interviewed; we apologise to those who might have made a significant contribution but who do not appear.

BOATS AND GEAR

In the 1800s, after rowing began to catch on as a competitive sport, more emphasis was placed on designs to make racing boats lighter, faster and more hydrodynamic. In 1846 Oxford began building outriggers on boats, allowing the oars to be attached further out from the side of the boat itself. This provided more leverage and stability, as well as the ability to make the boats themselves narrower and more streamlined. Early boats were also built from wood.

It was not until 1870, however, that the first sliding seats were introduced. This allowed for more rowing power to come from the oarsman's legs (most if not all rowers were men in those days), allowing nearly the whole of the body to transfer energy into the oar, and therefore the water. This advancement was mostly used in competitive racing vessels, with commercial or leisure rowboats still maintaining fixed-seat construction.

The club's first recorded purchase of a boat was in April 1864, when the 8-oared boat, *St. John of Malta* was bought for £10. It was used by the club constantly, until finally broken up in 1877. In the same April, however, a Mr. Hodgson was paid £6 for repairing this boat and for providing four new oars. That month, records also show that the boat station was removed to Port Royal for the princely sum of 3s. 6d (about 17p). The club members were clearly proud of their new boat, as they had the club's initials painted on the stern of boat for 14s (about 70p).

In 1868, a Mr. George Ross and three of his 'cronies' determined at all costs to obtain a four in which they might stand a chance of racing against other clubs. A four-oared boat was heard of in Plymouth, on sale for £20; the four friends raised £10 between them, the club funds providing the rest, and the *Amateur,* or 'White Boat' as it became known, became the club's second boat. It was thought that the boat was however rigged the wrong way for turning, which meant they had problems on short courses with bends, as on the Exe by the quay. The third boat, *Psyche,* another four, was bought soon afterwards, in which a successful crew was eventually trained.

Mr. Ross showed his enterprise again in 1871, by purchasing a 'skiff' called the *Southampton* for the club, for £5. Mr. Dart's history claims that *'it*

Photo 1: Skiffs in 1924 at the Port Royal

was peculiar that there was no definite notice of skiffs (at the club) until 1883' even though the club clearly had two such boats, *Southampton* and *Reply,* since 1871 and 1873. This may be because there were so few boats around that there were no opportunities for racing them. But these skiffs clearly attracted the attention of members, to the exclusion of other types of boats.

The term 'skiff', originally a Scandinavian word for a boat, has been used for a number of styles of craft round the United Kingdom, often small, river and sea-going craft. They varied from double-ended rowing boats to small sailing boats. There are references to skiffs on the River Thames (as a result of accidents!) as early as 1812, and in Oxford from 1824. However, in rowing terms, a skiff came to mean a single sculling boat. In Dutch and German, "Skiff" also means a single scull, while the Czech word *Skif* refers to sculling boats in general.

In 1876, the club purchased a canoe for £4, and further canoes were bought at various intervals in the coming years. It seems that canoeing was then considered to be just another branch of rowing, as the club got involved in many canoe races down the years. Unlike now, where canoe and rowing clubs coexist quite separately.

The next four-oared boat the club purchased was the *Spinaway* in 1876, for just over £13. This was the beginning of a period when a lot of new boats were acquired; no less than ten new boats in five years. These included the skiff *Isca* in 1878, a pleasure boat and a dinghy, both un-named, in the same year; and in 1880, the club's first two pair-oared boats, the *Fly* and the *Undine,* for £13 6s 7d. These were the first boats to be built for the club by Claspers (later Clasper, Salter & Kessell, of Plymouth), who provided the club with several new boats over the next decade.

In 1880, a quote was also received from Messrs. Stockham & Pickett of Southampton for a new clinker-built 4-oared boat complete with 'paddles', cover etc. and gold and blue beading. The quote specified several options for the construction, as follows:

Built of pine with mahogany fittings	£30
Built of cedar with mahogany fittings	£32
Built of pine without paddles or any fittings	£25

It seems that the cheaper option was agreed on, as the payment for the boat was just over £27. This new 4-oared clinker-built boat was named the *"Exonian"*. Two further pair-oared boats with paddles were offered to the Club in July of the same year for the sum of £12.10.0. plus the cost of railway carriage from Plymouth, and it was agreed to purchase them.

A year later, it was resolved that a '4-oared outrigged gig' be bought from Mr. Edwards for the sum of £5.

Like the term skiff, gig could have meant various things at that time. In the late 17th century gigs were working boats in the South West and the Scillies, ferrying pilots out to incoming vessels to help them navigate through the rocks and safely into harbour. The boats competed to get their pilot out to the boat ...and the fee...first. Gigs also served other purposes along the English coast; salvage, smuggling and lifesaving - sometimes under sail but more often rowed by a crew of six. Gigs needed to have length, lightness and flexibility to be manageable in extremely heavy seas. Gig racing was born out of the competition to get pilots out to boats and from the testing of newly built gigs against others to measure their performance.

In 1881, the club obtained a new outrigged four named '*Amateur*' after the old boat of that name, for £5. The price indicates that this could not have been a new boat, though it is not stated as to where it came from. (Quite often, the source of new boats is not disclosed in the club's records). The following year, it was resolved to have slides put into the *Amateur* and the secretary was empowered to order the same to be done forthwith, the cost not to exceed £3. This is the first record of sliding seats in relation to the club's boats, and must have seemed like a great leap forward.

There then seems to have been several lean years for the club, as only one new boat was purchased between 1881-1886, a boat named *Southampton* or *No. 16*. There seems to have been little appetite for competition during these years. Some members took advantage of this slump in competition to press for other kinds of boats, including dinghies and 'Oxfords' as they were then described.

But things began to pick up again in 1886, when it was resolved that Kessell Boat Builders of Plymouth be asked for their best terms to build a 4-oared inrig boat, 36 ft. long, built of cedar, with sliding seats and swivel rowlocks. A sum of £25 was later agreed following several letters between the club and the builders. This new four was to be named *Psyche* after the popular four that the club had had since 1868. A dinghy and a skiff were also bought that year.

In 1887, the club had a strong membership and successful crews, so that the introduction of double sculling races was considered for the first time. 1888 saw the revival of the Exeter Regatta, and there was serious competition in the fours, though ERC came through with first and second places. A new four, the *Ormonde,* was bought, and it was agreed that the club's stock of boats, now numbering 16 in all, be insured for £300, instead of the previous £250.

In 1889, the committee agreed that three skiffs and one Oxford be built by Mr. Edwards at a cost not to exceed £40. And in 1890, they also resolved that *'the Hon. Secretary contact Messrs. Clasper, Salter and Kessell for a price for a new 4-oared, sliding seat, swivel rowlocks boat, 36ft. 6in. long, overall width 2ft., in cedar wood'.* Mr. Kessell told the committee that he could build a gig and have it ready in about a month for £28. This was agreed to by the committee. The boat was called *Amateur,* to commemorate the club's first-ever four, bought 11 years earlier.

The Club now had five 4-oared boats; two pair-oared boats; seven skiffs or canoes, and five Oxford pleasure boats. It is interesting to note that the club had not purchased an eight since its original boat in over 25 years; clearly, rowing in eights was not popular in those days. Another new Clasper-built 4-oared boat was then bought in 1892, to be called *Spinaway,* again reinstating the name of the much older boat of the same name.

The new insurance policy to be taken out with the West of England Insurance Co., involved insuring the boats for £500, a big increase in just five years. This could be seen as down to inflation; but in fact there had been very little increase in boat prices in almost thirty years. The first four -oared boat in 1868 had cost just £20; in 1886, a similar new boat cost just eight pounds more, and in 1904, forty years after the first boat was bought, the price of a new four from Clasper's had only risen to £37. The 1893 Inventory of the Club's property was as follows:

5 4-oared boats

7 skiffs

5 dinghies

1 canoe

1 pair oared boat ("useless")

'Paddles ' - 3 sets for fours, 7 pairs for skiffs, 4 for dinghies, 7 for sculls, for the canoe

Cushions, including 18 short ("worn out in 1892")

2 sponges ("very dirty")

The existence of all those cushions is a good reminder that sitting in a boat has never been a comfortable experience!

1893 saw the purchase of two more boats: the four *"Why Not"* for £4, and four Southampton skiffs at £6 10s 0d each, all from Mr. C. Edwards. The inventory of the Club's property had now increased as shown:

5 4-oared boats (4 slides and 1 with fixed seats)

1 4-oared boat (for "Gig – Punt")

11 skiffs (2 very bad)

5 dinghies

1 Canoe

Paddles: 4 sets for 4s; 2 odd ones for 4s; 7 pairs for skiffs; 2 dinghy sweeps; 4 dinghy sculls; 1 canoe paddle; 2 boat hooks.

Cushions: 5 long; 2 long for canoe; 26 small (6 poor);

100 Books of Rules; 5 starting flags; 1 Mahogany box; 23 runner towels; 1 oil can; 1 sponge.

This had been a period when the club had experienced plenty of success in competitions. But as had happened before, things seemed to decline

Photo by   FOUR-OAR BOAT "MINNEHAHA."   *Heath & Braduce, Exeter*
R. H. Dymond (Stroke).   W. Webber.   W. S. Goff.   J. B. Holden (Bow).

Photo 2: Minnehaha

again in the years from 1893, even though new boats continued to be purchased. These included two skiffs in 1894, and two more in 1895, though these were not new boats, judging by the price paid.

Records of club activity seem very sparse around the turn of the century, and in his account, Mr. Edwards, a club member who was elected Chairman of WEARA in 1901, pointed out that there was 'no active rowing spirit prevailing' around that time. This may have been in part due to the Boer War, being fought in South Africa from 1899-1902, in which the Devonshire Regiment performed gallantly under Sir Redvers Buller, whose statue stands outside Exeter College. It may have been that club members were engaged in this war: a memorial to the 250 Devonshire Regiment soldiers who died can be seen in the cathedral.

No more boats were then bought for a period seven years. in 1904, a new racing four was ordered from Clasper's at the cost of £37, towards which members of the Club had guaranteed £20, and Mr. J. Gidley had offered a cheque for the balance of £17. The new racing four was christened "Minnehaha" by Mr. John Gidley and at the Exeter Regatta that year, it won the newly-awarded Morton Cup, the crew being J. Holden (bow), J.C. Voisey (stroke), W. Webber and W.S. Goff. They captured the trophy again the following year in *Minnehaha*, R.H. Dymond

Photo 3: The Excester at Double Locks

replacing Mr. Voisey. *Minnehaha* is also the first boat of which the club has a clear photograph, to be found originally in Mr. Dart's book.

But all boats were not as lucky or successful as this. The four named *Exonia* was considered to be 'unlucky', for example, though reasons are not given for this. The boatman at the Port Royal, Mr. Edwards, was recognised in 1905 by being given a permanent increase of £5 to his expenses for accommodation and care of the club's boats.

This was followed by the purchase of two dinghies in 1905, and some new equipment, including rowing mats, long cushions, three pairs of long skiff paddles, three sponges, and six bath towels. Six towels amongst a large-ish club seems to imply that members were expected to provide their own. And in the same year, the city council helped by installing a trolley and rails at the double locks to help move boats across the locks. The remains of the rails are still visible today.

In 1907, committee resolved that Mr. Lavis of Exmouth be approached to build a dinghy on the lines of the oldest dinghy in the Club at a price not exceeding £13.0.0, and they also recommended the purchased of more gear, including four more pair skiff paddles, one rowing mat, three cushions, three cushions be re-covered, four sponges and six more bath towels. Whoever was responsible for club kit at this

BOATS PURCHASED BY THE CLUB, 1864-1914

Year	Type	Name	Cost	Maker
1864	Eight	St. John of Malta	£10	-
1868	Four-oared	-	£20	R. Southcott
1868	Four	Amateur	£10	-
1868	Four	Psyche	-	-
1871	Skiff	Southampton	£5	-
1873	Skiff	Reply	£5	-
1876	Canoe	-	£4	-
1876	Four-oared	Spinaway	£13 2s	-
1878	Pleasure boat	-	-	-
1878	Skiff	Isca	-	-
1879	Dinghy	-	-	-
1880	Pair-oared (2)	Fly Undine	£13 6s 7d	Clasper, Salter & Kessell, Plymouth
1880	Four-oared	Exonian	£27 2s	Stockham & Pickett, S'ton
1881	Canoes (2)	-	£7	-
1881	Dinghy	-	£10	C. Edwards
1881	Outrigged four	Amateur	£5	-
1883	'Southampton'	No. 16	£5	-
1886	Four	Psyche	£25	Clasper, Salter & Kessell, Plymouth
1886	Dinghy	-	£10	
1886	Skiff	-	£5	-
1887	Four	Ormonde	-	-
1889	Skiffs (3)	-	£40	-
1890	Four	Amateur	£28 6s 6d	Clasper, Salter & Kessell, Plymouth
1890	Dinghy	-	££10	
1892	Clasper-built four	Spinaway	£46	Clasper & co.
1893	Four	Why not	£4	Edwards
1893	Southampton Skiffs (4)		£26	Edwards
1894	Skiffs (2)	-	-	-
1894	Punt	-	£3	-
1895	Skiffs (2)	-	£12 10s	-
1902	Skiffs (2)	-	£16	-
1903	Tub pair	Patience	£21 10s	Salter Bros, Oxford
1904	Clasper-built Four	Minnehaha	£37	Clasper & co.
1905	Dinghies (2)	-	£18 10s	Gann & Palmer, Shaldon
1907	Four	Exonia	£37	Clasper & co.
1907	Dinghy	-	£13	Lavis, Exmouth
1908	Tub pair	-	£21 10s	Salter Bros, Oxford
1911	Dinghies (2)		£28	Lavis, Exmouth
1912	Four	Excester	£76 15s 9d	J. Sims of Putney
1912	Dinghies (2)			Lavis, Exmouth

Photo 4: Mrs Pyne christening the City of Exeter in 1922

time clearly took their job very seriously! The committee also resolved that as the sum of £15 had been guaranteed by members of the Club, a new 4-oared racing boat be purchased forthwith from Mr. J. H. Clasper. This boat was christened the 'Exonia', and cost £37.

Another tub pair like the *Patience* was purchased in 1908, again from Salters of Oxford, but in the next few years, records show only more purchases of minor items of gear- cushions, towels, sponges and lockers for the changing rooms. It was not until 1911 that two more new dinghies were purchased from Mr. Lavis of Exmouth as per his specification, at an estimated £28 for the two boats. Club membership at this time had been gradually declining; from over 100, it had slipped to 84 in 1911.

In 1912 Messrs. Sims of Putney again supplied a new four and paddles at a cost of £39.10.0., and G. W. Lavis supplied 2 dinghies at a cost of £28. The name of the new four was the "*Excester*". The boat was made of cedar, 36 ft. long, with a beam of 1 ft. 11.75 in., the first centre-seated boat the Club had bought. The funds for the boat were raised almost entirely by the efforts of the members.

It was soon after these minutes of 1912 that the two histories of the club already referred to were produced. Mr. Dart's book, *'A short rowing history of the EARC'* appeared in 1912, and that by Mr. Edwards shortly afterwards. As already mentioned, these two sources have provided much of the information for our story so far: from here onwards, we are indebted to the club's records, which vary in detail from time to time.

And of course it was not long before the outbreak of WW1, when rowing virtually ceased and records were unavailable. The next evidence does not appear until 1920, when the club bought 14 pairs of new paddles for over £27, from Ayling and sons.

1922 then saw the purchase of two new boats, the first for many years: a gig from Ayling and sons for £7, and four-oared gig, to be called *"City of Exeter"*, with oars, for £85 in total, plus rail freight charges from Putney of £7. 13s 3d. The new boat was christened by Mrs. Pyne.

Two years later, at a boat sale, the following boats were purchased:

Double skiff	£ 5.15.0.
Single skiff	4. 0.0.
Single outrigged skiff	2. 5.0.
Double ourigged skiff	3. 5.0.
3 pairs 10ft paddles	2. 5.0.
3 pairs 9ft paddles	2.17.0.

The club must have been doing well at this time, as the following year, they purchased four more second-hand skiffs and four paired sculls from a Mr. Bartram for £ 53. 0.0. In 1928, the Captain reported 'he had arranged to have the three best dinghies scraped and varnished and put in good working order, together with one of the tub pairs'. The cost, including storage, would be £12. He stated that the tub pair was in need of a great deal of repair, but that Mr. Gregory had agreed to thoroughly overhaul it for the sum of £4. Mr. Gregory had bought the club's single outrigged boat for 30s. and the double outrigged boat for £1. A Mr. Sellick wished to have the dinghy at £1. The small dinghy was badly cracked and not worth repairing. Mr. Gregory also wished to have some odd blades at 2s. per blade and it was agreed he could have half a dozen "as the club could easily spare them".

So there had been a good deal of buying and selling of boats in the early 1920s. But by 1929, it was pointed out in the minutes that the newer of the racing fours was seven years old while none of the boats that their opposition were using were more than two years old. *'It was con* *imperative therefore that the Club should raise money for a new boat'.*

However, it was not until 1931 that an order for a new four was placed with Messrs. Sims of Putney at a cost of £76, to be christened *"Exon"*. The boat was actually delivered in July 1932, and christened *Exceter'*, and with oars, cost £ 95. 4s 9d.

There is now a thirteen-year gap in the records, from 1933 until after WW2 had ended. Minutes of May 1946 indicate that the boats and equipment had been insured for the sum of £2000 with the County Fire Assurance Co. It is likely that the club's stock of boats was by then pretty old, as there are no records of new boats being bought during the thirteen years since the arrival of *Exceter*. The first racing four was not purchased until 1949, and was christened "Port of Exeter". We do know, however, that this boat gave good service, as it was not dismantled until 1971, 22 years later.

ERC's first recorded eight was purchased around 1950 from Hereford, for £15 and was originally owned by Caius College, Cambridge. This boat was used on Opening Day that year and was rowed from Countess Wear to Turf, with Club officials making the journey in the Council barge. Later, in 1955, an ERC crew in this boat won the Lord Desborough Trophy for eights.

The *"Elizabeth II"* purchased in Coronation year was an 'unlucky' boat, like the earlier *Exonia*. Even today, there are boats which crews like and those they don't, even though there may not be any obvious reason for the difference.

But as the *Elizabeth II* was not popular, a new 36 ft fine racing four was commissioned from Messrs Sims of Putney and Hammersmith in 1955. A deposit of £52 10s was paid in December. A new type of blade with hardwood backs were to be ordered for this boat. The new boat was ready on 21st August 1956. Mrs Swain should christen it, she being instrumental in the commencing of the boat fund. The Christening took place in 13th Sept 1956, and the boat was named *"Walter Dorothy"*, in recognition of immense and invaluable contributions this member has made to the club. In 1957, a Tub and a fine four on order from Messrs. Holmans of Exmouth were now complete except for the supplying of the riggers from the manufacturers.

An enquiry was received from RAF station at St Eval for a second hand fine four in 1957. The secretary was instructed to reply offering the 1932-boat *"Exceter"* complete with rudder and swivel rowlocks for the price of £30. The sale took place in 1958.

i0s then saw yet another revivial in the club's fortunes. ist of £210 was ordered, the new racing four *"Ernest* ened in 1962 at the club's headquarters at the Port g to see how the price of a new boat had risen over years. Prior to that, prices had changed little in over 70 years; now, for the first time, boats were costing well into three figures. In September 1964, for example, another new shell fine four, costing £300, was delivered. The minutes mention that *"Any donations are welcome."* This was followed by a further purchase, the *"City of Exeter"* bought for £256 4s 8d., and in July, 1965 by the *"Marcus Hodges"* christened by Mrs. Hoare, the wife of the Club president. This newest racing four was 36 foot long, made of mahogany ply and cost £320. Blades were bought at a cost of £37. The new boat had a slightly modified shaped bow to make it faster.

March 1966 was notable for the fact that the club's new boat (purchased from Clifton College, Bristol), the *"John Percival"*, arrived. The local press carried the following item about the new delivery:

> *"ERC's bid to break into national class competition gets a boost this week with the delivery of a new boat. It is an eight – the first the club have owned in more than 10 years - and is being purchased from Bristol's Clifton College. Until now whenever they wanted to practise an eight race the club members have had to borrow a boat from the University club."*

A subscription list was started when the new purchase was announced and immediately nearly half of the cost was promised, mainly from rowing members. The purchase was followed by that of a third eight, the *"D. B. McNeill"* from Southampton University.

In March 1966 there appeared to be a Trust Fund Gift to provide new boats. It was reported that:

> *"ERC (1864-1966), literally riding on the crest of the waves during the past two or three seasons, can now look forward to a new boat every two or three years thanks to the generosity of one of its keenest vice presidents Mr Geoffrey Pring. The future is bright for ERC, doubly assured in fact by this latest very generous gesture by Mr Pring who was warmly thanked on all sides last night."*

David Macklin reported that he had been able to obtain a grant from the Education Committee for 50% of the cost of a new boat and it was agreed that another new boat be purchased, quotations having been obtained from all of the leading boat builders. Following this process, it was agreed that an order be placed with Richmond Racing Boats.

The new Boat, the *"Geoffrey Pring"*, a racing four, was christened by the Mayor of Exeter, Alderman M. Nichols, in May 1967 and launched in a ceremony at the clubs HQ at the Port Royal. The £400 boat was bought through the trust fund set up by Mr Pring, one of the Club's Vice Presidents and a longstanding member. In the same year, Marcus Hodges, Senior Vice President of ERC, re-christened the racing four *"Semper Fidelis"* which the club had given to Exeter Canoe Club and which had been converted into a K4 racing four canoe.

Another new boat, for which we don't have a name, was also purchased that year for £390.00, and two skiffs bought from Eton College boat house for £275. They were named the *David D. Macklin,* and *Andrew B.*

Despite this flurry of buying, the records in 1969 suggest that the club needed new boats, the current cost being in the region of £450, and sets of 4 blades at £50. In October 1970, therefore, a deposit was paid for a new boat of £100. The Ministry of Housing and Local Government granted the sum of £299 towards the estimated cost of £590 required for the new boat. And with the *"splendid response from the President, Vice Presidents and members"* it was now thought to be possible to purchase the boat. New blades were required at a cost of £70, which was the next

Photo 5: "John Ibbett" at Double Locks replicating the St John of Malta

target.

The new 42ft racing four was christened by the wife of the Club's President, Mrs. R. W. Pyne, at the Club's Port Royal HQ and one of the most closely guarded secrets among the members was revealed when she named the boat *"Len Rey"*(as seen on the front cover!). The boat cost £541.50;   of this £100 came from the club accounts and £170 from the New Boat Fund, the balance being the grant from the Department of the Environment.

An Eight Oared Boat Fund was also started in 1971. The fund was started early in the season when it was realised the present eight, the *John Percival,* purchased second hand in 1966, had done good service and was due to be "pensioned off". The *"John Percival"* was offered for sale by ERC the following year, and as replacement, the *"Shadowfax"* eight was bought from Selwyn College, Cambridge.

The records now indicate more purchases ahead:

> *The Eight Fund, having been successful in securing the new eight, is now concentrating on acquiring coxless pair boats. When the final list of subscriptions has been realised for the Eight Fund, any balance available will be allocated towards the purchase of the pairs.*

To make room in the boat house, the "John Percival" VIII and the "Walter Dorothy" IV with blades were sold to the newly formed boat club of Plymouth Polytechnic College.

What actually happened, however, was that the club agreed to proceed with an application to purchase one coxed four, 2 pairs and 1 tub pair. The Club had £256 in hand, including £36 from 'waste paper collections', and £70 had been received from St. Luke's regarding the purchase of the old four, *"City of Exeter"*. In 1974, therefore, the new coxless four *"Sir Gawaine"* was put through her paces. The new eight purchased by the fund was finally christened in 1976 at the Port Royal by President Edgar Lee, the boat being named *"John Ibbett"*.

Prices now really began to escalate. In June 1978, for example, a new boat christening at Port Royal attended by the Mayor and Mayoress was for a carbon craft, 45ft. long, costing £2,300. This newest boat was named *"Muriel Toy"*. So by 1981, the club's inventory of boats was as follows:

Eights: "John Ibbett", "Shadowfax"

Fours: "Muriel Toy", "Len Rey", "Marcus Hodges", "Ernest

Marks", "Geoffrey Pring", "Gawine" (sic), "Monks Justice"

    Sculling craft: "Ikarus", "Vesta 66", "Denys"

    Training tub: "Teacher"

Purchase of a fun boat was agreed at a cost of £464.31, and this was delivered in June 1983. In November 1984, the club bought a boat from Christchurch Rowing Club, the *"Swansea",* thanks to the Geoffrey Pring Fund.

In 1986, the AGM reported that there had been some good second hand purchases – fours, pairs and an eight – and that the Club would be purchasing a new lightweight four in the Spring. The Club had also been able to buy a new set of 12 blades for the regatta season through the generosity of one of the Vice Presidents. A 'job lot' of boats was purchased from Stourport Boat Club (an eight, three 4s, and a coxless pair, all needing some attention). A new boat trailer was purchased costing £1000.00.

A year later, the main acquisition was the four *"Pam Baker"* which arrived ready for the regatta season. The new lightweight boat was

Photo 6: Christening of Nick Parkin – Crew of Nick Parkin, Ray Grigg, Fred Stevens, Mike Curtis with Brian Sculpher and Paul Wilson

purchased with a grant from the Sports Council, an interest-free loan from the City council, and a generous donation from Mike Baker. The following year, the AGM reported that a new eight from Branston would soon be on the water. It is not made clear what this boat was to be called. However, in 1989, it was suggested that in future, the 15 year-old four *"Sir Gawaine"* should only be used coxless because of the danger to coxswains in the event of a capsize. Later that year, the AGM reported the biggest expense had been the refurbishment of the *"Pat Smart"*. There was a boat-naming ceremony for the Carbo Craft - *"Owen Burridge"* and the *"Instyle Eight"*.

In 1992, a new Janusek four was commissioned by the club, at a cost of £6,500. During the year, one of the women rowers, Georgina Robinson, a physiotherapist, was killed by one of her patients. As a consequence, the new four, suitable for a 13.5 stone crew, was named after her in 1994.

The last wooden boat bought by the club was also purchased in 1992 and christened *Nick Parkin*. This boat was with the club for a couple of years until, after an accident it was sold to Exmouth.

A new eight was also acquired in the summer of 1994, and later in the year, a set of four Dreisieggacker blades were bought from the University of London for £514. In July 96, the club purchased a new coxless pair that could accommodate both light and heavyweight crews. It was to be used for crews of Senior B status or above.

1998 saw an Aylings 8+ purchased, a 10 year-old boat from Reading RC for £800. It was said to be more suited to 11-13 stone rowers, the ladies being less suited to the boat, which was bought with sponsorship raised for the Atlantic Coast Challenge in which an ERC crew had come 7th. Two new sculls and a coxless pair were also purchased that year, as were two reasonably new ergos, saving the club £350. There must have been a big demand for training off the water, as another new ergo was purchased a couple of months later, for £500.

In early 1999, a new Janousek 4+ was purchased for £4000. The Instyle 8+ was to be refurbished, it was decided, at a cost of £1300, with £700 set aside for new riggers.

In 2002, a set of 4 blades was purchased 'so that the Club can boat a quad'. The first purchase of a cox box at £400 + VAT was recorded, and at the same time, megaphones for use by coaches, at £70 each, were obtained.

The following year, it was agreed with Pete Hogden that he would supply a new Stelph boat. The *"Pam Baker"* was to be rubbed down and re-varnished, and the runners on the *"Edgar Lee"* were pitted and needed to be replaced. In July, the blue Aylings scull had been purchased by the Club from the University for £200.

NEW BOATS PURCHASED, 1914-2000

1922	Gig		£7	Ayling & sons
1922	Four-oared gig	*City of Exeter*	£76	J. Sims & sons
1924	Double skiff		£5.15	
1924	Single skiff		£4	
1924	Single outrigged skiff		£2.50	
1924	Double outrigged skiff		£3.50	
1925	2nd-hand skiffs (4)		£45	
1932	Racing Four	*Exceter*	£95.4s.9d	J. Sims & sons
1949	Racing four	*Port of Exeter*		
1953	Coxed racing four	*Elizabeth II*		j. Sims & sons
1955	Fine four			J. Sims & sons
1957	Tub, and fine four			Holmans of Exmouth
1962	Racing four	*Ernest Marks*	£210	
1964	Shell fine four		£300	
1964	Four	*City of Exeter*	£256.4s.8d	
1965	Racing four	*Marcus Hodges*	£320	
1966	Eight	*John Percival*		
1966	Eight	*D.B. McNeill*		
1967	Racing four	*Geoffrey Pring*	£400	Richmond Racing Boats
1967	'new boat'		£390	
1967	Skiffs (2)	*Ikarus, Vesta 66*	£275	
1971	Racing four	*Len Rey*	£541.5s	
1971	Eight	*Shadowfax*		
1974	Coxless four	*Sir Gawaine*		
1976	Eight	*John Ibbett*		
1978	Four	*Muriel Toy*	£2,300	
1984	Eight	*Swansea*		

1986	Fours, pairs and an eight		All second-hand	
1986	An eight, three fours, and a coxless pair		All second-hand	
1987	Four	*Pam Baker*		
1988	Eight			Branston
1988	Carbo Craft	*Owen Burridge*		
1992	Four	*Georgina Louise*	£6,500	Janusek
1992	Four	*Nick Parkin*		Phelps
1994	Eight			
1996	Coxless pair			
1998	Eight		£800	Ayling & sons
1998	Two singles, one coxless pair			
1999	Four		£4,000	Janusek

Money for the naming of the boat the *"Mike Duff"* had been collected a while before, and it was agreed that efforts needed to be made to ensure that the Sims pair is re-named. An order was placed for the Women's 4+ and the 4x. The 'Wish list' of the Coaching sub-committee was then as follows:

3 sets of sculling blades at £250

Kingfisher pair

Weight bench with weights

LW scull at a maximum price of £1000

The two older ergo machines were to be auctioned. The funds raised by this auction would go towards the purchase of one "C" ergometer. Two other "C" ergos were donated to the Club – one by Mike Baker and the other from AMBA Marketing (Ruth Casson).

In 2004, the Coaching Sub-committee then agreed that pairs/doubles were the priority on the boat wishlist. It was decided to give the *"John Maxted"* to the South West Lakes Trust, and that a spares box would be set up with a spend of up to £1000. The Burgeshell single would be scrapped, along with the Kirton single. *"Denys"* was repaired, and was soon back in use.

In October, it was agreed that the Stelph 8+ should be replaced in January 2005 and that the Stelph 4+ should be replaced after the fours Head of the River. The *"Brian Sculpher"* was not being used and had been damaged twice. It was agreed that it would be replaced with a demonstration boat at 85kg. A month later, the Captain's report indicated that the plan was to replace the three worst wooden sculls *("Black Pig", "Denys"* and *"Ratty")* with new plastic training sculls at approximately £1,300 + VAT each, and to replace the *"Pam Baker"* (which had a split saxboard) with a second hand plastic IV at a maximum cost of £2,000. Then when funds became available, the club would replace the two Stampfli pairs with new plastic training pairs. It was also agreed that *'the juniors could name a boat if they raise enough funds'* (a precedent being the *"Little Devils"* named by the 1999 juniors).

The dedicated boats for the juniors would be *"Little Devils", "Pam Baker"* (or its replacement), and three sculls to replace *"Denys", Sims and "Black Pig".*

The Regatta committee agreed in 2005 to buy Jean Fentiman's scull for £500 and Rob Guegan's scull for £1,100. Purchase was agreed of a 75-85kg. 2x which was available at £6,500 including a credit of £1,000 from Pete Hogden from the sale of the eight+. £500 from the New Boat fund

Photo 7: The boats 2013

The current boat stock of the club

Boat Type	Boat ID	Make	Boat Name	Colour	Riggers Sweep / Scull	Average Crew Weight
1x	EXE 101	Janousek	Exe-tra small	White	Scull	75kg
1x	EXE 102	Janousek	Exe-calibur	White	Scull	75kg
1x	EXE 103	Olympus Sport	Exe and Bacon	White / Navy	Scull	85kg
1x	EXE 104	Janousek	Exe-tra large	White	Scull	90kg
1x	EXE 105	Olympus Sport	Exe Termi-nator	White / Navy	Scull	75kg
1x	EXE 106	Olympus Sport	Exe-Factor	White / Navy	Scull	75kg
1x	EXE 107	Stelph	-	Black	Scull	85kg
1x	EXE 108	Aylings	-	Blue	Scull	90kg
1x	EXE 109	?	-	Red	Scull	N/A
1x	EXE 110	Burgashell	-	White	Scull	65kg
2x	EXE 201	Stelph	-	Yellow	Scull / Sweep	90kg
2x	EXE 202	Stelph	-	White	Scull	75kg
2x	EXE 203	Stelph	-	Blue	Scull	65kg
2x	EXE 204	Aylings (Stelph)	-	White	Scull	75kg
2x	EXE 205	Janousek	-	White	Scull	65kg
2+	EXE 206	Wooden Pair	Robin Cave	Wood	Sweep	80kg
2x	EXE 207	Kingfisher	-	White	Scull	N/A
2x	EXE 208	Kingfisher	-	White	Scull	N/A
2x	EXE 209	Stelph	Pam Baker	Black	Scull	65kg

2x	EXE 210	Stelph	Mike Baker	Black	Scull	85kg
4+	EXE 401	Stelph	Brian Sculpher	Black	Sweep	90kg
4+	EXE 402	Janousek	Edgar Lee	White	Scull	75kg
4+	EXE 403	Janousek	Wyn Hitt	White	Sweep	65kg
4x	EXE 404	Stelph	John Ibbet	Yellow	Sweep / Scull	75kg
4x	EXE 405	Stelph	Ray Grigg	Yellow	Scull	90kg
4x	EXE 406	Stelph	Owen Burridge	Orange	Sweep / Scull	80kg
4x	EXE 407	Janousek	Little Devils	White	Sweep	65kg
4+	EXE 408	Janousek	Georgina Louise	White	Sweep	65kg
4+	EXE 409	Stelph	-	Yellow	Sweep	75kg
4+	EXE 410	Janousek	Steve Charles-Davis	White	Sweep / Scull	?
4x	EXE 411	Rossiters	-	White	Scull	N/A
8+	EXE 801	Stelph	Russell Andrews	Yellow	Sweep	80kg
8+	EXE 803	Eton Racing	High Performance	White	Sweep	75kg
8+	EXE 802	Empacher	Nottingham	Yellow	Sweep	85kg

was used to bolster the £1,500 from the regatta to purchase a new sculling boat. A grant application had been submitted to Sport England in the 'Awards for All' scheme by Don Fraser for a replacement Kingfisher double training scull, and the Club purchased a Stelph 2x from Pete Cork for £3,500.

A run-down of the recent purchases, made in September 2005, was as follows:

New equipment purchases:

2 x Double	£6,500
Junior 4+	£2,000
New Stelph 8+ and 4+	£3,000
White Stelph 2x	£3,500
Jean Fentiman's scull	£ 500
Robert Guegan's scull	£1,100
3 x Ergos	£ 265
2 x Ergos	£1,187
Free weights and wooden weight discs & clips	£ 417.50
4 x tressel sets	£ 315
Cox box	£ 200
Boat ties	£ 80
Barbecue	£ 635

Boat maintenance totalled £2367.14. It was also agreed to purchase a second hand Ladies IV at a cost of £3,000, and two cox boxes (£350 each), 5 sets of weights (£100 each), 2 life jackets (£75 each) and 2 walkie-talkie sets (at a cost of £49.95 each), all of which would come from the New Boat fund.

In 2006, there was a proposal that the Stelph Quad (which was apparently hardly used) was sold for £3,500 and a 70kg. Stelph 4+ purchased for £5,500 in its place. The new coxed IV arrived in time for the South Coast Championships. The "*Pam Baker*" was finally sold to Alasdair Stuart for £50 in order that it may be restored at Eton. It was resolved that a record for each boat would be compiled including information such as purchase price, wins, etc and damage would be recorded also. Sadly the records since then are a little sparse.

BOATS AND GEAR

Thanks to Dan Rowse for this inventory of the club's boats.

SOCIAL FUNCTIONS

Social events have always played an important part in generating a sense of solidarity within the club, and these have taken many different forms over the years. They include such events as the Opening Day; Smoking concerts; the Annual Dinner and Dance; the Vice President's Supper; skittles matches; picnics; days out on Dartmoor; Children's parties; Christmas activities; even an annual cricket match at one time. There have also been social activities shared with other local clubs, such as the famous 'Three Inns Run', and Swan's Nest cross country run.

Opening Day

Opening Day was held each year for many years, usually at either Turf, Double Locks or Starcross, usually in late April or early May. Ladies Days were also held. The first of these Opening Day events seems to have taken place in 1887, when a letter from Mr. Pearse at Turf offered *"to put on a good tea for the members"* on Opening Day, at two shillings (10p) each.

Opening Day in 1893 and 1894 included a row to Turf and tea as usual, whilst in 1898, the Opening Day involved a 'smoking concert' at the Port Royal on the members' return.

By 1899, however, the event had returned to the Turf, the cost of tea 'not to exceed 2/3 (11p)'. It is also worth mentioning that Sunday rowing was not allowed until 1896, and 'smoking in club boats' was only allowed below Countess Wear. Though how people could row and smoke at the same time is baffling!

By 1902, the Opening Day with tea was provided at the Courtenay Arms, Starcross. A launch was engaged to carry members from the Port Royal to Starcross, along the canal we presume, then through Turf Lock. This must have been a success, as it was decided to go to Starcross for Opening Day again in 1903. This time, however, the club members asked the railway company to supply a train to Starcross for Opening Day, also that *'a pianist be engaged for the same occasion'* (not from the railway company!).

Starcross remained the venue of Opening Day for the next four years, though transport arrangements seemed to vary. In 1904, for example, 80 tickets for Opening Day were issued, and the Hon. Sec. was asked to write to Messrs. Ellett and Matthews *'informing them that a large boat*

Photo 1: Opening day 1948

to be towed by the steam launch would be required and also a man to steer the same'. For the next three years, at the same venue, it was resolved that the amount of the expenses incurred for the Opening Day did not exceed 19 shillings (95p).

In 1908 Opening Day returned to the Turf. This time, the Opening Day committee engaged the 'council barge' for the day at a cost of £1.7s 6d (£1.37p). Mr. W. Hannaford offered the use of a horse for towing the barge along the canal on Opening Day free of cost and this was accepted with thanks. It was later reported that about 80 took part. The *Western Times* reported that:

> *The weather was fine but with a strong head wind and there was a mishap when the junior crew upset their boat when getting into it for the return journey and all went into the water. Fortunately they could all swim!*

A smoking concert was then held at Double Locks (see below).

Opening Day continued to be held at Turf for several years after this. In 1910, it closed with a concert at Double Locks at 9 p.m. Each subsequent year, plans seemed to develop in more detail; an

Entertainment Committee was formed, and by 1912, each committee member had to be responsible for providing a prize for the Opening Day events. The number present that year was 94, a record. After paying all expenses there was a balance of £2.12s.3d, *"this being the first Opening Day on which funds had been added to the Club".*

For the 1913 Opening Day, members left Port Royal at 2.30 p.m. by the Council barge and other boats, with games and other amusements to be arranged and tea provided at Turf at 5.30 p.m., the price of a ticket being 2/6 each (12p). The Newsletter reported that despite very unfavourable weather, the day was a great success. The accounts show a balance of £2.3.9. in hand after paying all expenses. This format was retained in 1914, except that two additional tow boats had to be engaged. Sports events were dropped and *"amusements of a money making character only be adopted"* instead. The day showed a profit of £4.6.2., to be handed to the Treasurer. The Newsletter asserts that the *"Big attendance testified as to the popularity of the Day."*

The council barge was not hired; instead the members, as far as possible, proceeded to Turf in the Club's boats. Tickets cost 2/6 (2/- to be paid for tea per head). Opening Day accounts showed a profit to the Club of 6/10.

Photo 2: At Port Royal with some pre-smoker smoking

As a consequence of WW1 and the lack of club activity, Opening Day was not held again until 1929. In that year, it resulted in a sum of £2.1.3. being handed to the Treasurer, all expenses having been paid. A photo had been taken at a charge of 1 guinea (£.1.1.0.) and it was agreed to arrange for different terms in future if possible. Just what 'different terms' meant is not clear; but there are few records of Opening Day events after this year.

Smoking concerts

"Smoking concerts, for which the Club proudly boasted a formidable array of talent among its members, were the acme of enjoyment."

Exactly what went on at these very popular events is not entirely clear. They were held mostly at the Port Royal from 1896 until WW1, with just two other subsequent events, in 1928 and 1947. For the first event in 1896, it was hoped all members would endeavour to attend, and in 1897, for the smoking concert at the Port Royal, a pianist was hired. This suggests that members (men only at this time) smoked, drank and sang to the piano.

By 1906, the "Smoker" as it was now called, again took place at the Port Royal, *for members and friends to wind up the season'*. And in the following year, a joint "smoker" was held with the Exeter Harriers Club at Port Royal. Edwards also reports that a 'capital concert and dance' was held at the Barnfield Hall in 1907.

By November 1911, the smoking concert had moved to be held at the White Hart; it was a busy year for social events, as many functions and competitions were arranged, including 'illuminated concerts' at Double Locks, which were very successful, and an 'entertainment' at the Theatre Royal. In 1912, the concert also involved the presentation of wedding gifts, Club Sculling Championship medals and skittles prizes, again at the White Hart, and a 'Gramophone Recital'. The club's first Billiards Handicap was held, and a skittles tournament at Double Locks.

This however is the last mention of such events until 1928, when one more "Smoking" was to be held at the White Hart. The only subsequent reference is in 1947, when a 'supper and smoking concert ' was to be held.

Annual Dinner/Dance

This has been a feature of the club's social calendar since 1882, and continues today.

In the early years, the venue fluctuated between the Bude Hotel and the Globe Hotel, neither of which exists any more. In 1882 and 1883, at the Bude Hotel, "*tickets were not to exceed 3/- each*" (15p); and this price and venue seems to have been sustained until 1890. We have no more records of the annual dinner until 1898, when it seems to have moved to the Globe, and the price of the tickets had risen to 3/6 "*inclusive of waiters' fees*". The Globe seems to have continued to be the favoured venue until 1904, when the event reverted to the Bude Hotel, though it was back at the Globe for 1905, then to a new venue, Mr. W. H. Morton's hotel, referred to in Edwards' history as The Turk's Head, in 1906. For several years after this, right up until WW1, the venue seems to have alternated between the Globe and the Bude, with the price somehow having been held constant at the original three shillings. Inflation must not have been a problem in those years! However, in 1909, it was resolved that no dinner be held this year for some reason.

The 50th anniversary celebration dinner at the Globe Hotel was attended by 97 members,

And was later reported as being "*most successful*".

But from then until 1920, no dinner was held during and after the war years. In 1920 it moved back to

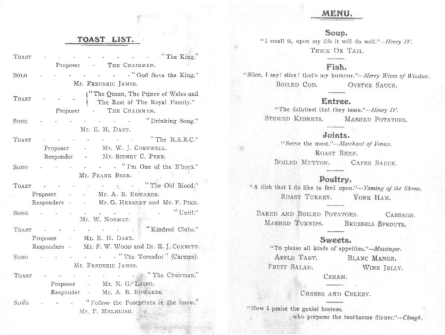

Figure 1: The toasts and menu from the 50th Anniversary Dinner programme

the Bude Hotel, when the *Western Times* noted that:

> *"A very popular pre-war practice was revived by the E.A.R.C. when they held their annual dinner in the Bude Hotel."*

By 1928, it became referred to as the 'Annual Ball', and would be held at the Rougemont Hotel on 16th November, with the Ted Meads band. The following year, the Treasurer reported that the annual dance had been a great success from the point of view of the members, but the financial result was not so acceptable, there being a deficit of 13s.6d.

The secretary reported that a profit of 1s.6d. (just 7p!) was made at the annual dinner (held at the Bude Hotel in February), which would be increased to 18s. as three members were unable to attend but had offered to pay for their tickets.

In 1929, the Royal Clarence hotel became the venue for the first time. There was a choice of a 4s. or 5s. Menu. This seems to have been repeated until 1932 at the Royal Clarence, when it continued to be well attended. No records of the Annual event exist however from then until 1950, when the first post-WW2 dinner was held at the Crawford Hotel. However, making a profit on the event seems to have continued to be a problem. In 1951, for example, the profit from the last dance was just 15/3 (78p). In 1952 and 1953, the event moved again, this time to the St George and Dragon Hotel, at which 85 attended.

Then in 1954, the club tried out the Wingfield Park Social Centre. Tickets were now 6s 6d (32p), and 80 members attended, though this does not seem to have been a success, as the following year, it moved yet again, this time to the Countess Wear Hotel, prices being increased to 12/6d for members, rowing members 10/6. Despite the increase, the dinner again made a net loss of £7 17s 4d, mainly due to the issue of 10 complimentary tickets.

Ticket prices went up again next year, still at Countess Wear, to 13/6d. The 1957 event commemorated the 21st anniversary of the chairmanship of Mr. A. J. M. (Marcus) Hodges who joined the club in 1928, was Chairman of WEARA 1939-1947, and life member of the National Rowing Association.

The next records relate to 1964, when the Centenary dinner was attended by the Mayor of Exeter and his Mayoress, the Sheriff of Exeter and his lady. The Newsletter says of this event,

"What more appropriate to the occasion could be a toast to those 'Old Timers of the river' – Walter Dorothy and Ernest Marks – and to the youngest members present – Charles Kerslake and Leslie Moyle."

In 1965 and 1966, the event was still held at the St George and Dragon Hotel, attended by 84 each year. Tickets were a guinea each (£1.05p). Then in 1967 the event moved to a completely new venue, the Langstone Cliff Hotel in Dawlish Warren, at a cost of 24/6 not including coach transport. It continued to be held here until 1972, the price rising gradually to 32s 6d (£1.62p). 1971 still had a record attendance, despite rising prices.

The following year saw another change of venue, and more price hikes. This time, the event was at the Chevalier Hotel, and was well attended. By 1974 the cost was £3.25 (decimal currency had been introduced the previous year) and in 1975 the Annual dinner/dance was at Winstons. Tickets were £3.25 (dinner only £3.00). It continued to be held at Winstons until 1981, when the tickets now cost £7.50, and was attended by over 100 people. In 1979, the dinner/dance at Winstons was combined with the WEARA President's dinner, and was attended by 165 people from across the region.

The 1982 dinner was attended by 80 at Reed Hall, but in the following year it moved to the Rougemont Hotel in October, and remained at this venue until 1986, when the price rose for the first time in six years, to £8.50. In recent years the annual dinner has been held at the Rougemont, Reed Hall and at the Exeter Chief's ground, Sandy Park.

Vice Presidents' suppers

This event has been variously known as Committee Suppers, Vice President's Suppers and, currently, President's Suppers. These have certainly been held since the end of WWII and were originally held at the Port Royal before moving to the Ship Inn in Heavitree as well as other locations. These suppers were very strictly "males only" evening, with women grudgingly allowed to attend with the election of Mrs Toy as President in 1974. The suppers continue as President suppers and for the past few years have returned to the Port Royal.

The attendance seems to have averaged around 30 members, and was almost always held in Heavitree at the Ship, though in 1970 it was held at Gypsy Hill, and there were usually two or three such suppers each year. In 1971, the records indicate that, bizarrely, *Christmas wrapping paper was on sale for 2p per sheet in aid of the Boat Fund'.* And in 1972, there was a raffle in aid of a children's party, which raised £2.80.

In 1980, the event moved to Winstons, then to the Prospect Inn in 1982. Raffles became a regular feature of the supper by 1987, when the event was held at the White Hart and raised £37. In recent years the supper has been held at the Port Royal, one time home of the rowing club.

Skittles matches

Skittles matches were regularly held over many years. Like the Vice-President's Supper, there was usually an element of fund raising attached to these events, either by a raffle or entrance fees. In 1912, such a Skittles' evening was held between married and single teams and was won by the married team. In the 1960s, the event seemed to be held about four times a year, mostly at the Swan's Nest. However, in 1972, there was a *'Skittles, dancing and buffet' night* at the Farm House Inn, Exmouth. It then became the norm to hold the matches at the Ley Arms, in Kennford, until 1983 when it switched to the Coaver Club at County Hall, followed one year by 'dinner at Quo Vadis' in Heavitree, and another year by a barbecue at the Boathouse. The event seems to have attracted around 40 members. The club continues to hold informal skittles matches with a makeshift alley and skittles and balls made by one of the members.

Children's parties and other activities

Children's parties at Christmas were a regular feature from 1965 for many years and included a visit from Father Christmas with a present for each child. Father Christmas was usually played by one of the members and resulted in such questions as *"Why is Brian dressed as Father Christmas?"!* They were often combined with a bazaar or "fayre" in the attempt to raise funds. The parties were arranged and catered for by Mrs. Toy and the Ladies section. We know that they continued until at least 1984, and in 1971, the party was attended by 50 children, whilst in 1980, the bazaar raised £60.

In 1965 there was a club Carol service at St. Mary Arches Church attended by around 70 members and friends; and the following year, 1966, ERC took a party to the pantomime at the Princess Theatre, Torquay. This was repeated in 1967 with a visit to see Dick Whittington at St. Luke's Theatre, followed by refreshments at Wingfield Park.

In recent years the club has hosted a Christmas Dinner and raffle, usually catering for more than 60 members in the club house with a meal

Photo 3: Christmas dinner 2013

prepared by senior members of the club.

Other ERC Activities

In August 1900, it was decided that a Club picnic be held on the canal on Saturday, 18th August. The Picnic was a success, as it was repeated the following July at Turf. Sports were held at the picnic.

1912 saw the first club 'Day on Dartmoor'. It seems to have been a very wet day and about as bad as it could possibly be for the Moors. Despite that, 24 members turned up at Queen Street station and a very enjoyable day was spent, the best being made of the unfavourable circumstances. An excellent tea was held at the Dartmoor Inn. The Dartmoor Quartette(sic) also sang and *"assured us in a key as horrible as the weather that they were jolly good fellows et cetera"*. It was suggested that another trip be held at a later date and that the Hon. Sec. *"be instructed to obtain a supply of 'bottled sunshine' for this occasion"*.

Members must have enjoyed the day despite the weather, because "Another day on Dartmoor was thoroughly enjoyed by a party of 16 and the weather was good in comparison with our previous walk."

In 1913, it had been resolved that a 'Ladies Day' would be held, and this event first took place in July 1914. Ladies Day was reported to have been a great success, although owing to the small numbers present , a greater cost to the Club had been entailed than expected (viz. £2.19.9.). "Tea to be had at Turf at 6 o'clock, with sports and amusements to be held on the green before tea." A concert was held at Double Locks on the return journey. Prices of tickets (to include refreshments at the Locks on the way back) were single at 3/- each and double at 5/6 each. Numbers were limited to 50, "a number the barge will take with comfort".

The first Annual cricket match was held at Double Locks in 1928 (presumably on the small grassy area where people now play volleyball) and it was agreed that a tableau would be arranged for the St. Thomas Carnival. However, this only seems to have happened once, as the club decided It was unable to participate in the Carnival the following year.

1946 was the year in which the Michaelmas draw was discussed. It was suggested that the prizes should be 12 geese, plus poultry etc. It was also agreed that a 'tripe supper' should be held at Port Royal before Christmas, limited to 30 attendees.

The 'Goose Draw' was repeated the following year, and it was anticipated that it would show a profit of between £40 and £50. 1953 saw the first Regatta Dance, held at the Civic Hall, which was hailed as a great success, the net profit being £61. And importantly that year, the Social committee decided to open the club one evening a week from 7pm - 10pm. There would be table tennis, darts and rings, as well as refreshments by the Ladies section!

Marcus Hodges had been a stalwart of the club for many years, and so at a commemoration dinner at the Countess Wear Hotel in 1957, he was presented with a silver tankard to mark his 21 years as chairman of the club. It was kept as a complete surprise to Mr Hodges that he was to be awarded this silver tankard.

1966 saw the first Darts match at Port Royal, and others followed. There was also a football match that year, in which ERC played a 'Dolphins XI', losing 9-1. The Regatta dance was held at the Caprice, tickets 6/6 each. The club clearly liked other sports to participate in; and having not been exactly strong at soccer, they took up tug of war. There were Tug of War competitions at Ide and in the following years, club members tried their hand at rounders, darts and soccer (again!).

Photo 4: D Manning, P Wilson and J Hammond compete in the pram race

In 1970 someone organised a 'ramble', everyone taking their own picnic tea, on the Hunters Path Walk from Chagford to Fingle Bridge, travelling by coach from Fish Quay to Sandy Park, Chagford and return from Fingle Bridge. Members paid 4/6 each. There was also an ERC Motor Treasure Hunt that year- these were very popular at the time- and in 1978, the first club disco, at the Admiral Vernon pub. Discos then seemed to be a regular thing, as they were held in the boathouse on regatta night and at Routes, then in 1982 at Boxes on the quay.

There was a party to celebrate Len Rey's 80th birthday at the Royal Clarence Hotel also in 1982, and Len and Nora celebrated their Golden Wedding anniversary with a rowing club party at the Coaver Club. Never short of ideas for fun activities, in 1989 the club competed in its first Pram race and held a Ceilidh in Boat House (tickets £2.50 each).

Activities with other Clubs

For a long time, there was a close relationship between ERC and Exeter Cycling Club. In 1893 it was resolved that the invitation of the Exeter Cyclists Carnival committee on behalf of the Devon & Exeter Hospital Saturday Fund to take place on Friday, 6th October would be accepted; and the following year, a letter from Mr. Burridge of the Exeter Cyclists Carnival committee stated that "*he had been desired to send the enclosed five recommendations for the Exeter Dispensary and two for the Homeopathic Dispensary in return for the part taken by the EARC at the last carnival*", also asking for a continuance of our tableau at the next carnival. The Hon. Sec. was to place a notice in the dressing room informing the members of both and that applications for the same be made to the Committee with a recommendation as required. However, ERC had reluctantly to reply saying that "*that the Club regret they are not in a financial position this year to send the usual tableau but wishing it every success*".

The club did however take part in the carnival in 1896.

In 1912, The Newsletter records that:

> *During the summer, interesting fixtures were held with Exeter Cycling Club at Turf and Double Locks, and in October, at the invitation of ECC, at their clubhouse, a splendid evening was spent, the Cycling Club favouring us with their company at our winter Headquarters at the latter end of November*.

A combined trip of EARC and ECC left Port Royal at 2.30 p.m.

> "*An enjoyable afternoon was spent at Turf with the*

members of the Exeter Cycling Club. Cricket and skittle matches took place between the two Clubs and also two novelty events. All were won by the Rowing Club."

Later that year, a cricket match was held between EARC and Exeter Cycling Club at Double Locks which EARC won by 3 wickets. And in the following year, the Cycling Club invited ERC members to join them at Double Locks when inter-club cricket and skittles matches would be held, with tea after, and in the evening an *'al fresco concert'*. The clubs got together again in 1914 for a 'programme to consist of a whist drive followed by a smoking concert'.

"During the evening Mr. E. H. Dart presented to the captain of Exeter Cycling Club on behalf of EARC club members a valuable and splendid flag. On rising to reply Mr. C. Harvey, captain of ECC, was visibly moved."

Cricket, skittles and "tea matches" between EARC and ECC at Double Locks continued throughout that year. EARC won the cricket and skittles, *"but the Tea Fight (?!) trophies were carried off by ECC."*

'Three Inns Run'

This event, from the Prospect to Double Locks and back to Port Royal, was run for the first time in 1964, the ERC Centenary year, and continued until at least 1985. It seems that about 25 members usually competed. Russell Andrews won the second run in 1965, however subsequent results are not recorded. After a break the event was resurrected in 2013 and the winner was Jonty Webber. The event must have been popular, as in February 1965 the club inaugurated another similar event, the 'Swan's Nest' Cross country run, four miles in total, attracting over 30 runners. This event continued until at least 1980.

The activities that the club engaged in have been many and various, reflecting on the way that, in earlier times, people had to make their own entertainment rather than relying on TV and digital media for this. Happily, many of the activities have survived in the club, a tribute to those who give their time to organise things'.

Photo 5: Three Inns Run

Photo 6: Swans Nest Run

WOMEN ROWING IN EXETER

The ERC Ladies Section started in 1950 although there is documentation of ladies sculling round the 1920 period. Ada Kite, in a piece in the *Express and Echo* in 1997, pointed out that that there was a Port Royal Ladies Racing Club, of which she was a member, in the few years before the outbreak of the second world war. They won many championships in West Country regattas, though never realised their ambition of beating the Torquay ladies.

Minutes of 1946 however suggest that there were to be no ladies' crews this year *'because of other commitments'*, though it is not clear what these were. In 1949, the men of ERC agreed that the use of the tubs be granted for a ladies race, *"but this should not be taken as opening the entry of ladies to the Club"*. Clearly, pressure was building up to allow women into the club, and in June 1950, the question of a ladies section was discussed for the first time.

This was obviously a very divisive issue at the time, as in July, the Club captain stated that he would resign if the proposal was carried, *'as the Club had no equipment to spare'*. This seems now like a flimsy excuse to keep the 'ladies' out; but it was at least agreed that the ladies could use the tub pairs only until the matter was settled. A resolution was passed that *'the ladies be allowed a probationary period to the end of the present rowing season'* and that they be allowed the use of the tubs when available, as well as one four when allocated. The ladies would put forward proposals at the end of the season to form a separate section with their own officers.

It was on 10th November 1950, therefore, that the first inaugural meeting was held to form a ladies' section and three of the key members were present ; Marcus Hodges, Chairman in those days, Sam Cuthbert, club captain for 1951, and Winnie Smart. The outcome was that a women's crew was formed and rowed in 1951. The crew consisted of Mary Symons (nee Gregory), Pam Westaway (nee Binding), Win Smart (nee Isaacs), Joyce Coles (now in New Zealand) and Ann Webber (nee Toy) as reserve.

The ladies then held a meeting and elected their officers and committee. It was decided to use funds to purchase a boat being offered at £20. The vote in favour of the formation of a ladies' section also

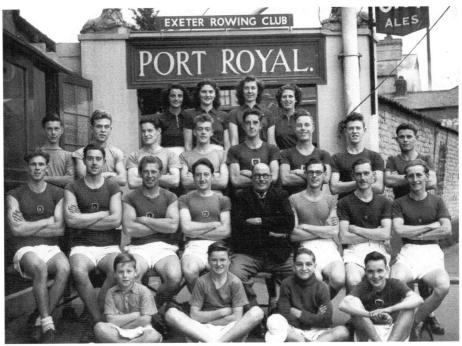

Photo 1: 1951 Club photo with first ladies

accepted that the section would be limited to 12 active members. Thus the Ladies Section of ERC was founded, under the chairmanship of Miss Hackworthy.

In September 1953, the Ladies four were WEARA champions. As a result of their success, they began raising funds and hoped to buy a four of their own, as they were still dependent on borrowing the men's four, and the two sections were still quite separate. There are no records of this boat actually being purchased, though it must have been, as it gave rise to an incident the following year. Minutes show there was a complaint from the Ladies section that their four, the '*Port 1*' was used by the men on an outing to Dawlish Warren and damaged. After interviewing the two crews which rowed to Dawlish that particular Sunday, it was decided negligence could not be proved. The use of the ladies' boat, it was claimed, '*was due to a misunderstanding by the captain*'.

There is little information on Ladies rowing for the next ten years. In 1964, the records of the centenary reception given by the Mayor at the Guildhall make clear that they were celebrating both the Senior Championship crew and the Ladies' Championship crew.

In 1971, the women's section of ERC held their 21st birthday celebrations at Wingfield Park social centre, Heavitree. The former

Photo 2: 1952 Ladies crew

chairman Mrs R. Moore cut the cake, watched by the first crew members of 1950. Records also show that the 1971 crew consisted of Marlene, Mary, Ann and Beverley. The Ladies', it was pointed out, had been successful in championships in 1953, 1954, 1956 and more recently in 1965. Their next Major success came in October 1973, when the ERC women's crew competed in the Ladies Head and finished 2nd of 21 crews, only 5 seconds behind the winners. A month later, at the Ladies Night at Wingfield Park, the 'A' WEARA and South Coast championship crew were entertained at the dinner by the Ladies section and congratulated on the season's achievements including the recent Ladies Head.

At the AGM of Ladies section in 1974, it was reported that the women had started a boat fund in order to replace their existing boat, now 20 years old. A jumble sale would be held at the Labour Hall, Clifton Hill, on 30th March to raise money for this fund. They also held a "Ladies section sponsored row' on the Exe (some 15 miles) raising nearly £100 towards their new boat fund.

Photo 3 & 4: 1971 21st Anniversary Celebrations

Later that year, an important milestone in the club's history was reached when, at the AGM of the full club, Mrs. Muriel Toy was elected as the Club's first lady President. ERC made history by electing the only woman rowing club president in the South West and possibly in the country as a whole. The impact of this was clearly important, as the following year saw the (inevitable?) merger of the men's section and ladies' section, the ladies becoming full members of ERC. This was a sign of changing attitudes in society as a whole, when 'women's lib' was a powerful movement. At the Guildhall, a reception was give for successful crews, including the Ladies 'B' crew, Junior 'A' crew, Veterans 'A' crew, Boston Marathon Senior 'A' crew and club officials. From here on, therefore, the story of the two sections becomes one: and forty years on, the women's section thrives as well as, if not better, than the men's.

CUPS AND CHAMPIONSHIPS

In its 150 year history, the club has competed in a wide range of competitions and championships, and won quite a number of cups and trophies, many of which have been presented by club members or local people of importance. Sadly the whereabouts and origin of many of the cups mentioned in the records are unknown; however the following chapter gives some details on some of the key trophies. The first mention of winning a trophy predates the club's official existence, in 1846, when an Isca Four won the Dove Cup at Teignmouth Regatta in August.

The Dove Cup has something of a mythic status in the club. The unprepossessing Ceylon tea box that houses the Dove Cup also contains a copy of a newspaper clip, insurance valuation (£750 in 1950) and a letter to the club about the cup. The letter is dated 28th December 1939 to Marcus Hodges, and comes from the son of the original owner of the cup, a Mr. Lansdown Harding. His letter records that his father (who was stroke of the winning crew) had told him that the cup was won at Teignmouth Regatta in 1846 in a fours race between a Teignmouth and an Exeter crew. The Teignmouth crew were expected to win with ease: the Exeter crew allowed them to think they were favourites by keeping a little to the rear until they approached the end, where a strong spurt won it for the Exeter crew. The letter does not say, however who the other members of the crew were.

An *Express and Echo* article from 1940, meanwhile, reports on the return of the Dove Cup to Exeter through the donation of Mr. Harding. It also records that a *Western Times* article from the period reports that the race took place on 21st August and attracted four entries, for an amateur rowing prize of ten guineas given by the directors of the South Devon Railway Company, whose trains had brought some 3000 people to the regatta. The starts were reported to be the *Dove* and the *Ariel* (Exeter), against the *Sylph* and the *Anna Maria* (Teignmouth). The finishing order was Dove, Sylph, Ariel, Anna Maria. The losers, according to the newspaper article, *'expressed some dissatisfaction at the award, the Dove having rounded the mark on the wrong side and had only gone round once'*. The argument obviously didn't hold up, however, and the cup was named, the Dove Cup from then on.

The next mention of a trophy is in 1871, when the Exeter four competed against a four from Bristol for 'Four silver cups'. There is no mention in the records, however, of what these cups were called, and whether they still exist. But it is not until 1904 that the records mention another new trophy, the Norton Challenge Cup, formally presented to the club by a Mr. W.H. Norton in June. There is also a mention of a Morton Cup being presented in the same year, though it isn't clear whether one of these names is a mis-spelling. The winners of the first Morton Cup at Exeter regatta was by a crew made up of Mr J. Holden, J.C.Voisey, W. Webber and W.S. Goff, in the *Minnehaha*.

A year later, Mr. R. Morris also presented two silver medals to the club, for the winners of the senior and junior championships.

Exeter's silver collection, housed in the Guildhall, pays host to a large trophy won outright by members of the St Thomas Rowing Club in 1909. The Lile cup was won by the same crew three years running and as such retained by them. Following the decline of St Thomas Rowing Club the crew members, W and A Dorothy and E and W Marks came, eventually, to Exeter Rowing Club

Photo 1 & 2: The Dove Cup

One of the problems in writing the story of the club's trophies is that while we have names of various trophies, evidence is often lacking regarding what they were presented for. An example of this is the Duke Cup, first presented in 1911: a committee of four members was elected to decide on how it should be awarded, but the records don't tell us what the cup was for.

Photos 3 & 4: The Lile Cup and the winning crew in 1907

However the Blanchford Cup, first awarded in 1913, was for an 'open handicap sculling race' to be held annually. The current Blanchford cup was presented to the club in 1932. The Vulcan Goblets were also competed for in this year, the condition of retaining the goblets being that they must be won twice in succession or three times in all, before becoming the property of any member. They were eventually won outright by the Pyne brothers in 1932; later, the brothers donated the trophy back to the club to be rowed for as the Vulcan Pairs trophy, which dates back to 1913.

These trophies continued to be competed for at least until 1928. At this time, the records from the Regatta programme provide us with a list of all the trophies currently competed for in the club.

Name of Trophy	Donated by	Value
The Newman Bowl	Sir Robert Newman	22 guineas
The Owen Bowl	Sir James Owen	22 guineas
The Plummer Challenge Vase	E. S. Plummer	150 guineas
The Orchard Challenge Cup	J. H. B. Orchard	25 guineas
The Cornish Bowl	F. Cornish	15 guineas
The Crosse Shield	Mr. & Mrs. S. E. Crosse	10 guineas
The Blanchford Cup	F. Blanchford	6 guineas
The Hibberd Shield	W. D. Hibberd	10 guineas
The St. Thomas Challenge Cup	Trustees of the late St. Thomas ARC	65 guineas
The Bruford Challenge Bowl	Wm. Bruford & Sons Ltd	40 guineas
The Wippell Shield	J. Wippell & Co. Ltd.	20 guineas
The Lisle Cup	Messrs. W. J. Lisle & Sons	8 guineas

Sadly, the records again have little information on exactly what races each of these cups related to or their current whereabouts but the Lisle (not to be confused with the Lile Cup!) Cup is still awarded by the club for senior sculls.

1957 was the next year in which we have evidence of new trophies. A Mr. Bill Gorphin of Exmouth was keen to promote the idea of a *'Head of the Exe'* race, and along with other leading Exmothians, donated a silver cup, the *'Exmouth Townsman's Trophy'* for the race, first held on May 25th that year, from Port Royal to the Exmouth Coastguard station (where the old lifeboat house was, next to the new bowling alley). Sadly the trophy was won by another club, possibly in the 1990s, and hasn't been seen since.

Many of the club's trophies are still displayed in the clubhouse. There seem to have been quite a few trophies (see below) for 'cross country events' as well as for rowing! These may have been the races mentioned in an earlier chapter, where competitors in canoes paddled down the river, shot Trew's Weir, carried their boat 'cross country' to the canal, and rowed back up to the winning post. The latest inventory was made in 1967, when the Newsletter carried the following lists:

Trophies and Cups for present day events within the Club:

Dove Cup (outstanding achievement; not awarded every year). Recent recipients include Melanie Moore, Peter Cork, Lisa Souch, Marcus Bowyer and Julia Wood.

J.H.Lile Cup (under-18 fours champions)

Lisle Cup (senior sculls)

Rowsell Challenge Cup (Junior doubles)

Conneeley Cup (Novice champions)

Victor Ludorum (Club with most points in the regatta)

Harry Ehrens Perpetual Cup (personal achievement by 1st year oarsman)

Muriel Moore Perpetual Trophy (personal achievement by 1st year female oarsman)

Frank Ward Perpetual Cup (team award in 3 Inns cross country)

Bowman Junior (M. C. B. Hoare) Perpetual Cup (individual award in 3 Inns cross country)

P. K. J. Smart Perpetual Cup (lady's award in 3 Inns cross country)

Marcus Hodges Perpetual Cup (coxswain's award in 3 Inns cross country)

Macklin Trophy Perpetual Cup (team award in Swan's Nest cross country)

Rey Trophy Perpetual Cup (individual award in Swan's Nest cross country)

Exmouth Townsman's Perpetual Cup (Head of Exe race)

Photo 5: The Victor Ludorum

Trophies of interest donated to ERC
Silver sculling model from Port Royal ARC
1883 Silver salver (Mr. M. R. H. Guyver) per 'Isca B' Club
1846 Silver cup from Lansdown Harding
1800 Regatta gun from the Literary Society
1907/08/09 Silver Miniature Senior 4s (late Alfred Dorothy)
Blanchford Cup from Port Royal ARC
President's medallion from M. T. Baker
Case of model boats from St. Thomas ARC to P. Royal and ERC

Championships won by ERC over the years.

As mentioned above, the first victory recorded by an Exeter club was at the Teignmouth Regatta in 1846, when a four won the Dove Cup. In 1874, a Mr. F. Pike appears to have won *'more prizes than any other club member'* but we don't have specific details of these victories. However, between 1879 and 1893, the club records do show that ERC was pretty successful in local regattas, as follows:

1879: Firsts at Starcross, Torquay, Totnes and Dartmouth.
1880: Firsts at Starcross, Torquay, Totnes (2) and Bideford (2).
1881: Firsts at Torquay, Totnes (2), Bideford (2).
1882: Firsts at Bideford and Teignmouth.
1883: First at Bideford; four firsts at Exeter.

In his account of the club up to 1912, Mr. Dart says that *'this was a good five years' work, but it was seen that competition fell flat in 1883 and 1884, this being the usual experience after a run of luck on the part of one particular club.'* We were clearly the club to beat, in those years. But support definitely weakened at this time, as records show that the club didn't compete in regattas for several years, until 1887, when an influx of new members seems to have rejuvenated the club somewhat. Still, as late as 1890, it was 'regretted' that no regular records of club successes in away regattas had been kept.

However, there are some records for the period 1890-1898, and during that time, the club gained the following successes in our own Exeter regatta:

Senior fours:	two firsts and four seconds
Junior fours:	two firsts and one third
Senior pairs:	one first, five seconds, one third
Junior pairs:	one first, two seconds, two thirds.

The following years enjoyed numerous successes but sadly we only have the most basic information about championship successes, as follows:

Championships during 105 years of rowing in Exeter

St. Thomas ARC (disbanded in 1921)
1896 Junior Champions
1907 Senior Champions
1908 Senior Champions
1909 Senior Champions
[Crew: A. Dorothy, W. Dorothy, E. Marks, W. Marks, with various coxes]

Port Royal ARC (formed in 1927)
1929 WEARA Junior Champions
1931 WEARA Junior Champions

EARC
1908 WEARA Junior Champions
1921 WEARA Junior Champions

Photo 6: Club Photo 1975/76

1922 WEARA Junior Champions
1932 WEARA Junior Champions
1946: EARC and Port Royal ARC amalgamated
1949 N.A.R.C. Junior 4s Championship of all England.
1951 WEARA Junior Champions
1951 WEARA Novice Champions
1953, 1954, 1955 WEARA Champions
1958 WEARA Ladies Champions
1962 South Coast Junior Senior Champions
1963 WEARA Ladies Champions
1964 WEARA Senior Champions
1964 WEARA Ladies Championship
1965 WEARA Junior Champions
1966 WEARA Junior Champions
1996 Men won Junior Senior South Coast Championship
1996 Ladies won Senior South Coast Championship
1996 Ladies won Junior South Coast Championship
1996 Men won WEARA Senior B Championship
1996 Ladies won Senior A WEARA Championship
1996 Ladies won Senior B WEARA Championship
1996 Ladies won Senior C WEARA Championship
1970 WEARA Senior Champions
1973 WEARA Ladies Championship (A crew)
1973 South Coast Ladies Championship (A crew)
1974 WEARA U18 Champions
1974 WEARA Ladies Championship (A crew)
1975 WEARA Ladies Championship (B crew)
1975 WEARA Junior Champions (A crew)
1976 WEARA Senior Champions (A crew)
1976 WEARA Junior Champions
1976 South Coast Open Ladies Champions
1979 WEARA Senior A Champions
1979 WEARA Senior B Champions
1980 WEARA U16 Champions
1981 WEARA Senior A Champions
1981 WEARA Senior C Champions
1983 WEARA Novice Ladies Championship shared by ERC and Reds
1984 WEARA Novice Ladies Championship
1986 WEARA Novice Mens Championship

The club has gone on to achieve many successes in recent years, as described by various individual contributors in other chapters. For example, in 2008 the IM4+ crew of Dave Parsons, Russell Barrowcliffe, Andrew Woolley and James Webber, with Christian Wilmington as cox, won the Boston Marathon by a margin of 1hr 15 minutes. Had they been entered in the correct category (Novice 4+) they would have set a course record for novice fours. The men's squad at that time also won three 4+ categories at WEARA championships in 2009; the J16 and J18 girls squads were also very successful in those years.

In 2013 the Ladies squad won the WEARA Novice Womens 4s Championship. A title that the Ladies have successfully competed for numerous times over the years. Also in this year Daniel Willmington won the WEARA senior A and B championship and Imogen Mackie won the WEARA J18 sculls.

In the latest year, 2013, the club has had successes with men's and women's squads and individual scullers. The tables below summarise these wins.

Photo 9: 2013 WEARA Novice Ladies Squad

Sculling successes, 2013

REGATTA/HEAD RACE	EVENT	WINNERS
Gloucester Head	WIM3 1x WM 1x Women's novice 1x	Eleanor Burke Julia Wood Anna Newton
Totnes Head	WMD 1x	Julia Wood
Evesham Regatta	Women's Master's 2x Women's Master's 1x Men's J16 1x	Eleanor Burke/Lucinda Sanders Julia Wood Andrey Kontyaev
National Master's championship	WMB 1x WMC 1x WMD 1x	Eleanor Burke Julia Wood Julia Wood
Monmouth Regatta	WIM2 2x Mens J16 1x	Eleanor Burke/Lucinda Sanders Andrey Kontyaev
Totnes Regatta	WJ15 1x Men's J17 1x Men's Senior A 1x Men's Senior B 1x Men's Novice 1x	Poppy Bowyer Andrey Kontyaev Dan Wilmington Dan Wilmington Arved Schwendel
Wimbleball Regatta	WJ15 1x Men's J16 1x	Poppy Bowyer Andrey Kontyaev
Henley Women's Regatta	Women's senior 2x	Eleanor Burke/Lucinda Sanders (qualified 10/26)
Exeter Regatta	Men's Senior A 1x Men's senior B 1x Men's Novice 1x	Dan Wilmington Dan Wilmington Arved Schwendel
Henley Master's Regatta	WMB 1x	Eleanor Burke
National Championships	WJ15 1x Men's J16 1x	Poppy Bowyer (15th) Andrey Kontyaev (20th)
Dartmouth Regatta	Men's Senior B 1x	Dan Wilmington
Bideford Regatta	Men's Senior A 1x Men's Senior B 1x	Dan Wilmington Dan Wilmington
World Master's Championships, Varese, Italy	WMC 1x WMC 2x	Julia Wood Julia Wood/Suzanne Hitchings (Dart Totnes)
WEARA Championships	Men's senior A 1x Men's senior B 1x Women's J18 1x Women's Senior C	Dan Wilmington Dan Wilmington Imogen Mackie Imogen Mackie

Men's squad successes, 2013

REGATTA	EVENT	WINNERS
Evesham Regatta	IM3 8+	Men's eight
Monmouth Regatta	IM3 8+	Men's eight
Exeter Regatta	Various	Victor Ludorum
Henley Royal Regatta	IM3 8+	Qualified, lost to 4th seed crew
Dartmouth	Senior A 8+	Men's eight
Totnes Head	Novice 4+	Men's four

The South Coast Rowing Championships Regatta

The South Coast Rowing Champions was the inspiration of Archie Fraser of Westover & Bournemouth Rowing Club who had the idea of an event involving the three South Coast Rowing Associations – the Hants & Dorset ARA (H&D ARA), the Coast ARA (CARA) and the West of England ARA (WEARA) – who would provide a champion in each class to compete in a "champion of champions" race at the end of the rowing season.

The first Championship Regatta was hosted by H&D ARA at Poole in 1957 where Christchurch were the winners of the first Senior event. The following day officials from the three Associations met in Poole Yacht Club where it was decided that the regatta should continue and be hosted by each association in rotation.

In the early years there was a good deal of controversy between the associations because of the different rules and because WEARA rowed in 36 ft river boats (now 42 ft) instead of the 30 ft staggered coastal boats used by the other associations. However annual meetings of the South Coast Council have now established a set of acceptable rules and regatta format. The original three year cycle was changed to a four year cycle with the regatta being held in WEARA every other year to counteract the disadvantage that WEARA crews suffered from having to row in coastal boats. The three year cycle was re-instated in 2011. In 1967 it was stated that the cost of staging the South Coast Championship Regatta was £270 – today it is around £25,000.

Although the supporting events had often included ladies 'Open' races these was no Championship event for the ladies until 1976 and in 1992 a Junior Ladies Championship was added, with a Veterans Championship added in 2004 bringing the total of Championship events to six.

Exeter has competed at the Championship since 1958 representing WEARA 62 times and winning many times making them the most

Photo 8: 1974 Ladies Crew (Marlene Ramsden, Bev Hill, Ann Dallen, Mary Tuckett) taken in 1973

successful WEARA club in the Championship. The best year came in 1996 winning the Junior/Senior Championship and both Ladies Senior and Junior Championships. Exeter's wins at the SCC over the years up to 2004 are as follows:

1962: Junior Senior fours. J Ibbett, N Parkin, D Hitt, B Sculpher. Cox: L Moyle

1973: Senior Ladies open event. B Hill, M Ramsden, M Tuckett, A Pallen. Cox: S Ibbett

1974: Senior Ladies open event. B Hill, M Ramsden, M Tuckett, A Dallen. Cox: K Hooper

1976: Senior Ladies fours. L Lakin, D Jonas, B Reynolds, M Heslop.

1988: Junior Fours. N Hitt, A Hopgood, S Aplin, S Midcalf. Cox: J Burrows.

1990: Junior/Senior fours: P Fitzhenry, N Fitzhenry, D King, C Casseldon. Cox: S Pike.

1994: Ladies senior fours. K Simons, M Aggett, A Dentith, K White. Cox: S Overall-Pike

1996: Junior/Senior fours. C Rogers, C Cockram, G Fuhri-Snethalge, J Prothero.

1996: Ladies Senior fours. E Pendle, K Abbott, A Nash, A Dentith.

1996: Ladies Junior fours. C Love-Jones, J Woods, F Peters, G Brown. Cox: A Stewart.

2000:Junior/Senior fours. M Robertson, D Haynes, S Power, J Copping. Cox: P Cork.

2004: Ladies Senior fours. M Moor, H Rawlings, P Bowden, R Painter. Cox: J Jacobs.

2006 Ladies Senior Fours P. Bowden, A. Kupschus, L. Souch, L. Cocks, Cox P. Cork

2006 Ladies Junior Fours J. Whistance, A. Dean, L. Souch, A. Nicholas, Cox P. Cork

MANAGING THE CLUB

There are many aspects to the running of a successful club over such a long period of time, the most important of which is probably a solid financial base, along with a strong membership, sensible rules and a code of discipline. Another aspect that binds a club together is its adherence to a club uniform, something that has changed over the years but is still important as a means of club identity. These matters have always been debated and still are, as evidenced by the current discussions on health and safety, capsize drills and safety boats. The following sections look at each of these areas in turn.

Subscriptions and other money matters

There are few references to accounts in the first 15 years or so, except that the subscription, in the first year, amounted to 15s 6d (about 77p). But from then on, someone kept excellent records. Financial success varied; between 1886 and 1906, for example, the annual balance was always in the black, though never more than £65 for any given year.

It was resolved in 1906 that,

> ' if the Club did not have a considerably larger balance in hand than £2.11.4., Mr. Charles Edwards of the Port Royal should be approached with a view to reducing the sum of £8 for rent, staging and care of the boats to the former amount, viz £3, at the end of the present season.'

In 1887, the rule allowing 'old active members' to pay just 10/6 p.a. (52p) after 7 years was rescinded: in the future, the rule would be that after 10 years successive membership the subscription for these members would be only 10/6. It was also agreed that after 01/05/1887 the entry fee would be increased from 5/- to 10/-. During these years, there was a constant refrain about members who have not paid their subscriptions, with letters being sent, names of defaulters displayed and, eventually, cancellation of their membership. Some things clearly have not changed in over 150 years!

In 1909, the Hon. Treasurer produced his statement of accounts showing that there was "an adverse balance due to the Treasurer of £22.9.6." by 1912, the Hon. Treasurer reported that he had the largest balance in hand during his 20 years as treasurer, namely £63.11.11' And yet a year later, the balance had dropped to a mere 6s.2d (about 31p!), and by 1914, the club had an adverse balance again, of £16.12.5 owed to the treasurer.

There was little activity during and after the war years, as recorded in other chapters; and by 1929 the treasurer stated that a Bank meeting had taken place, and that the deficit of £28.0.5. was being wiped out, leaving a balance in hand of £1.5.5. The depression years led to inevitably precarious economic times, and in 1930, the balance in hand was only £11.1.9.

And so things chugged along. Over 30 years later, in 1966, the club's balance was still only £317.5.4, with rent and rates totalling £80. And by 1971, this had risen to £707.24. (in 'new money' by then, of course!).

It does not make good reading to carry on reporting the year on year financial situation, except to say that, whilst things ticked over without too many crises, and the new premises finally came into being, by the spring of 1989 the balance was reported as "not too healthy". Just sixty members had paid their annual subscriptions and donations had been received from various Vice Presidents. This meant that there had to be many fund-raising activities in the form of the sale of Christmas cards, a draw at the Vice Presidents' supper, food sales at the Club house, and a sponsored walk when 15 members raised £300.

The club is currently experiencing a period of relative prosperity with a large number of members and even waiting lists for new members. Whilst these periods bring with them more income from membership they are accompanied by greater demands for equipment and higher maintenance costs. The lot of the treasurer, it seems, is never a happy one!

Subscriptions

In the current years when inflation makes prices rise year on year, it's easy to overlook the fact that, for many years, this was not the case. For example, the Club's annual subscription in 1908 was £1.05 (1 guinea) or 52.5p (half guinea) for juniors and novices; and this remained fixed for no less than 30 years! Entrance fees were also charged; these were 10/- in 1912 , but reduced to 5/- the following year.

In 1946, it was agreed that 'interested persons' could become Life

Members on paying the one-off sum of £5.5.0. (5 guineas). Subscriptions to ERC however were still only 10/- per annum for active members over 18 years of age, 5/- per annum for active members under 18, and 5/- per annum and for honorary members who would be non-rowing.

But by 1948, it was agreed that, in view of the Club now being open for the whole of the year, the subscription should be raised from 10/- to 15/-. This rose to 15s. by 1952 and 7s.6d. for juniors and novices.

Rises now became an almost annual event; by 1965 the annual subscription was £20, but in 1974 it fell, for some reason, to £19.50 (only a drop of 50p!), and records suggest that in 1975 the full members' subscriptions would now be a mere £5, Juniors £2, Associates £3 and school children and students £1.

In 1977, subscriptions were raised to £10 per annum, and this had gone up to £12.50, (U18s £5, those attending further education £2.50), by 1980. On the rises went; in 1981, subscription increased to £17, (U18s £10, Juniors £3), and by 1985, annual subscription was £20. Now, of course, the annual increase alone is more than this, an indication of the rapid rise in the cost of just about everything the club consumes.

Fund Raising

The ingenuity that has gone into fund raising over 150 years has been impressive and very necessary to keep the club afloat. It would be too tedious to list every event, but the range of ideas is long. Here are just some of the many things that have been organised over the years:

Whist drives and dances

Draws and raffles, including the 100 club

Tableaux in the carnival, and prizes won

Jumble sales

Sponsored walks (including a 24 mile event in 1969)

Donations

Monte Carlo Pinboard

Coffee mornings and suppers

Bazaars

A medieval banquet

Collections of waste paper

Collections of Green Shield stamps

Discos

A key time for fund raising was at the time of the 1979 ERC Building Fund. In addition to the Geoffrey Pring Fund, there were various donations from former members and the profits from the 100 Club draw which since its inception in 1973 had ploughed back over £1000. And with the current plans for a new HQ, fund raising has again become crucial .

Membership
This fluctuated in the early years, from as few as 30 in 1884 to as many as 79 ten years later. In 1895, there was 'room in the Club for 10 new members.' Yet In 1902, for some unexplained reason, the club decided 'that no junior members be admitted'. By 1904, however, membership amounted to 98 and it was resolved that this number of members be not exceeded for this season. The following year, Membership was limited to 100.

There is little record of membership in the war and inter-war years. The next information we have is from 1966, when active rowing members were listed as 13 Seniors, 5 Juniors, 3 Novices, 4 coxes (25 in all). The Ladies' section had 6 rowing members and one cox. In 1971, the list of rowing members had grown a little to Men 27, Ladies 6, Coxes 7, and remained fairly constant for several years, by 1974 being Men 28, Ladies 13, Coxes 3, 'Police 12 + 11 cadets'. It was not until 1983 that membership began to rise again, rowing members then totalling Men 33, Ladies 7, Coxes 3. The current membership has 12 life members, 111, adult members and 57 junior members. . All names of current (2013-14) members are given in the appendices'.

Club Rules and Discipline
The first reference to this in the club records is in 1881, when it is stated that '*a Book of rules be sent to new members*'. Ten years later, it was then agreed that 300 Books of Rules be printed for £2.10.0.

There is more in the records about rules being broken than about the specific rules themselves. For example, in 1892, there were complaints about a member:

> *having taken away an Oxford boat on a Friday night and kept it all day Saturday, without signing his name in the book.*

It was resolved unanimously that he be fined 3/6 (17p) 'which must be paid before he can again use any boat belonging to the Club'.

In the same year- there must have been a stickler about rules in the club at that time- It was resolved that

> *'the new four be not taken below Double Locks without the express sanction of the committee and then only by a recognised crew in training for a race'*

This new four would have been the *Spinaway*. A Rule Book, it was agreed, should be kept in dressing room and that *'all accidents happening to Club property be entered therein'*.

In 1894, a Mr. M. Hannaford got himself into trouble with the club, when he took a skiff to Exmouth and somehow damaged it. It was agreed that he be censured and fined 2/6 for breaking Rules 37 and 21, and that he must pay for the repairs. Also, it was decided that:

> *"Mr. Baker and crew who took away the 'Exonia' on Sunday, thereby breaking Rule 21, be fined 2/6 each".*

Clearly, the club disciplined its members quite severely in those days. For example, in 1896, it was resolved that a new rule be added to the existing ones, viz

> *"that members be not allowed to smoke in racing boats the Port Royal side of Countess Wear".*

Why anyone should want to smoke while rowing is strange, but clearly it was acceptable once you got beyond Countess Wear, for some reason!

In 1897, Rule 2 was also amended, to read *"The Club is to be limited to 80 active members paying one guinea per annum each."*

Members were reminded that they

> *'must observe the rule for entering their names in the Dinghy Book when taking the boats out, and if necessary this rule will be enforced by a fine'.*

In 1904, a notice had to be posted in the dressing room complaining about the neglectful way the skiffs were being used. And there seem to have been rules for just about everything, in those days. For example, in 1905, it was:

> *Resolved that the Hon. Sec. have a notice placed that three bath towels are missing and hope that the member who removed the towels from the dressing room will in future*

exercise more care in returning them.

Somebody probably still has them in their linen cupboard.

More seriously, there seems to have been an attempt to rig an election in 1906. It is recorded that:

> *"Mr. H. C. Gould asked the Chairman whether it is within his knowledge that an official of the Club has been approached by one of its members who threatened that unless officials' influence was used to compel certain members to vote in favour of the election of a certain candidate for membership and a promise to be given to that effect, all other candidates for membership would be black balled. This question ended in general disorder."*

It turned out to be a turbulent year for the club, as this was followed by Mr. W. S. Goff's resignation as secretary and captain. Mr. Goff was asked to give his reason which he did as follows:

> *"that owing to the action of certain members in preventing new members from joining the Club, the majority of whom would be rowing members, meant he had no other alternative than to resign his positions as secretary and captain of the EARC."*

His resignation was accepted.

Some rules, however, can only make us smile now. In 1908, for

Photo 1: 1913 Committee members

example, it was resolved that:

> ' the coxswains be allowed in the dressing room only to change their shoes'.

and that the minimum fine for any infringement of the rules be 2/6 (12p).

The archives contain a small Rule Book from 1953, when the club subscription was just £1, and ten shillings (50p) for U-18s. This rule book, however, is less about rowing than about the club's constitution, detailing offices, committee membership, joining the club, conduct of meetings etc. Only one rule mentioned boats, as follows:

> No boat shall be used except by the sanction of the Captain or his representative.

Joining the club seemed to be much more formal then than now: in order to join, the rules state, you had to:
'cause a notice in writing' stating your name, address, occupation, and age, to be forwarded to the secretary three days prior to the next committee meeting.
There was also pressure on committee members to turn up, as

> 'anyone absent from four successive meetings without informing the chair of their reasons shall automatically cease to be a member'.

Over the years the committee of the club has changed with new offices added to cover health and safety, welfare and juniors. In 1913 the committee comprised of seven members, all men.

100 years later the committee are more than double that with at least 16 members, a proportion of which are women and which also includes junior representation. Photos of the current committee and a list of post holders over the 150 years is included in the appendices.

Club Uniform

The club colours have seen many changes over the years. In an extract from Hon. Sec. ERC's report of 1868, the earliest reference we have on this, it states that

> "Members are reminded by Mr. Dicker that the uniform of the Club for the year 1868 was to be white jersey, white trousers, white boots or shoes, and cap, all new."

Quite what the cap looked like we do not know; but by 1881, records show that

> *'8oz. caps, blue serge with silk pipings, be ordered at 1/6 each (7p) from Mr. Edwards, the same to form from the time of their distribution among the members part of the uniform compulsory".*

The Caps cost 1s.6d., and badges 2s. (10p). The wearing of uniform was quite strictly insisted on, it seems, as a few years later, the secretary was instructed to write to Mr. W. Turner

> *'that he must wear the club uniform or the committee will be bound to take further action in the matter.'*

A new uniform was discussed in 1892 and samples requested. Prices quoted were as follows: straw hat 2/6, cap 1/6, vest 1/8, sweater 4/3, blazer 11/6, ribbon band for straw hat with badge ½ (one half of one penny!) Notices were put up in the dressing room informing all members that they

> *"must go for their Club uniforms to Messrs. Coles and Wittals of the Arcade where they will get it at the contract prices".*

By 1904, things were changing again. It was resolved that

> *'in future members in training for racing would be allowed to wear boots in the light racing fours instead of rubber shoes but must step into the boat with boots off.'*

1906 saw the introduction of the idea of 'Club Colours' as a mark of distinction. A motion was passed that:

> *' in order to encourage rowing amongst the members who represent the crews in various regattas, the members of the Committee shall sanction the wearing of "colours" (mauve) as a mark of distinction, the apparel of these colours to comprise blazers, caps and vests.'*

This change was formalised in 1912, when a Club championship badge was designed, to be a Maltese cross with a safety pin behind, to be engraved as shown:

Photo 2: A Maltese Cross pin

E

A   R

C

and in the centre circle, the inscription to be Senior or Junior Champion respectively with the year of winning same inscribed also.

Dart's history of the Club tells us that in 1912, the definitive uniform at the time was as follows:

> White vest and sweater with blue Maltese cross
>
> Blue cap with white piping and silver Maltese cross
>
> Straw hat with blue band and white Maltese cross
>
> Blue blazer with white braiding and Maltese cross

The date of the Club's foundation (1864) was to be placed on the badge under the Maltese cross. However, other records tell us that a '*definite shade of mauve*' was to be used for the rowing singlets, WEARA having decided that the Club should row in mauve.

It was not until 1946 that the club colours changed again. As WEARA had not approved the colour royal blue for the Club (as it was already allotted), it was agreed that green should be the main colour for ERC. Racing colours of the Club would be:

> *"mid green vests for first crews, mid green vests with white sash for second crews, with white shorts".*

This uniform was to be used by all oarsmen for racing or training. A Mr. Hawkins had obtained 15 shirts, 12 pairs of shorts and a coxswain's jersey (all second hand) for £3.9.0; and later, 25 racing vests were purchased at the price of 5/11 each.

In 1947, a drawing for a new Club badge was approved subject to obtaining the permission of the City Council for the use of the castle on the shield, which was received by the time of the meeting in February . This remained the uniform for 17 years. In January 1964, a new Club blazer badge became available at a cost of 43/-. (£2.15p).

And in 1969, a metal Club car badge (a replica of blazer badge) was supplied at 39/- each. In the early 70s, new rowing vests were now available at £1.25 each. Club ties, badges etc. were available – ties 65p, gold wire badges £2, track suit badges 37p, lapel badges 23p, plain green rowing vests 50p, trimmed white rowing vests £1.35.

In the 1970s lycra kit started to make an appearance and, for better or worse, this is now the ubiquitous material for kit with most choosing to train and race in all in ones. The new fibres and designs mean that we now have kit that keeps us warmer and drier than our predecessors and should make rowing more comfortable. However, inflation having its usual effect we now have rowing gear that costs:

All in one £46.50; Leggings £34; top £30; splash jacket £73.50 and hoodie £25.

For the anniversary year, replicas of the original uniform are being created for club rowers to wear.

Photo 3: 2013 men's squad at
Henley in current kit'

NOTABLE FIGURES IN THE LIFE OF ERC, THEN AND NOW

There have been many individuals who have made enormous contributions to the success of ERC over the years. Some have sadly passed on; some are still with the club after many years of service; others are recently arrived but still major contributors to the life of the club. The brief portraits in the first section of this chapter relate to just a few of the names that crop up commonly in the club records, on trophies or on the honours boards in the club house.

THEN...
Walter (Walt) Dorothy (1875-1970)

Walter was, in turn, a member of Exeter Amateur Rowing Club, St. Thomas Rowing Club, and Exeter Rowing Club, and was made a life member of each of these clubs. At one time, Walter was landlord of the Fountain Inn (now known as the Prospect Inn). His brother Alfred was landlord of the Port Royal and at some time of the Shakespeare Inn.

Photo 1: Walter Dorothy (centre left) 1956

In 1932, a presentation was made to Walter Dorothy in appreciation of his valuable service to the club. He was elected captain, and in April 1956, it was decided to name the new boat "Walter Dorothy", in recognition of immense and invaluable contributions he had made to the club.

A Press cutting: *('City Rowing Hopes')* 1959 has the following to say about him:

> "......*But the man around whom the officers claim the club really revolves is 84 year old Mr Walter Dorothy, its veteran member. Himself a championship oarsman in the*

1900s when he belonged to the old St Thomas ARC, Walter can now be found most days of the week busy doing maintenance work on the boats in the club house at The Port Royal, often accompanied by his dog, Whiskey."

Walter retired from active "boat care" in 1960, and died in February 1970. He was described as:

"A man who was associated with rowing in Exeter for 83 years has died at the age of 94... Mr Dorothy won his first race when only 11 years old in an Exeter regatta event. He and his brother Alfred excelled in pairs and were rarely beaten. He had almost the same success in fours with Alfred and the brothers William and Ernie Marks."

Ernest Marks (1883-1972)

Ernest Marks started his rowing career as a coxswain when he was a teenager and progressed to become one of Exeter's most outstanding oarsmen. In 1896 he coxed the Junior fours Championship crew of that year. In August 1909, he won the Senior Championship with his brother Walter and the brothers Alfred and Walter Dorothy. They won the Bideford Senior fours Championship trophy outright, which was presented to the City for custody and is now part of the City Silver Collection in the Guildhall.

Photo 2: 1962 Ernest Marks with the new boat

In 1962 a boat was named after him.

On his death, the press referred to him as:

'One of the best known personalities amongst rowing enthusiasts in Exeter and the West of England at the age of 89. The Marks brothers and the Dorothy brothers were an unbeatable force in their heyday at the turn of the century.'

Marcus Hodges (1904-1976)

A.J. M. Hodges was elected a member of the Club in April 1929. He was created a Life Member of ERC in 1947, after being chairman of WEARA from 1939 to 1947. He then became a life member of The National Rowing Association in 1957, and was Chairman of ERC for 28 years until 1964. Elected President of ERC in 1968 he became a Life Member of WEARA and Regatta committee.

Photo 3: 1965 Marcus Hodges (right)

In September 1957, at a commemoration dinner at the Countess Wear Hotel, Marcus Hodges was presented with a silver tankard to mark his 21 years as chairman of the local club. It was kept as a complete surprise to Mr Hodges that he was to be awarded this silver tankard. A press cutting at the time pointed out that:

"Mr Hodges is an engineer, following his father as head of the firm of that name at the city basin, Exeter. His interest in rowing began when he joined ERC as a 24 yr old novice in 1928 In a comparatively short rowing 'life' Mr Hodges has had his spills. Among the wettest was at Paignton regatta in his first year at the Exeter club, he was in the sea for 20 mins half a mile from land before being picked up by a motor boat.

His biggest surprise was the year he went with a scratch crew to Salford on a more or less social visit, and came back to the complete surprise of all with The Freeman Challenge Cup. 'It just happened that our method of starting suited the conditions' said Mr Hodges. They never lost their lead."

Marcus was also a tennis player and footballer and drove in car trials. A boat was christened in 1965 and named **Photo 4: Len Rey**

"Marcus Hodges" in his honour. He celebrated his 70th birthday in 1974 and retirement from active business commitments.

Marcus Hodges died in July 1976, referred to as *"Popular figure and personality at all regattas, whose valuable advice was constantly sought."*

Len Rey (1902-19?)

Len instituted and edited the ERC newsletter for many years. He was President in 1973-74, Social Secretary of the club for 21 years, and General Secretary of Exeter Regatta for 15 years. In 1977, he retired from the committee and was elected Life Member. He has been described by many as 'a real gentleman'.

In April, 1966 he was presented with the Embassy Award for being the *"Sportsman of West of England who had done the most for the well-being of any sports organisation in the area"*.

In October 1971, the new ERC 42ft racing four was christened by the wife of the Club's President, Mrs. R. W. Pyne, who named the boat Len Rey, members having decided that this was a fitting way to repay him for his hard work. He became President of ERC in 1974, and on 18th August, 1982 Len's 80th birthday was celebrated at the Royal Clarence Hotel, when a presentation was made to him.

Len took it upon himself to be the club's record keeper: this book would be much the poorer if he had not done this. He also produced an invaluable 'scrap book' of photos and cuttings, which has been used extensively in researching the book. He was always at the clubhouse, and started the 100 club. Nobody ever said no to him, for the simple reason that he did so much himself, and was widely respected across WEARA.

Muriel Toy (?-1985)

In 1973, Muriel Toy was elected Chairman of the merged Ladies' and Men's sections; and a year later, at the club AGM, she was elected as the Club's first lady President. ERC made history by electing the only woman rowing club President in the South West and possibly in the country as a whole.

Photo 5: Muriel Toy

122

Photo 6: Pat Smart

Patrick (Pat) Smart (?-1987)

Pat spent much of his life on or around the waters of the Exe, and he served the club and the city for many years, including as President in 1986-87. In 1948 he was a member of the club's first-ever tideway eight, and in the following year joined the junior four that won the All-England Junior Championship. He became Club Captain in 1954, and during his second year as Captain, represented Exeter with Owen Burridge in the West of England eight that won the coveted Lord Desborough Cup. In 1994, as a boy of 14, he had won the Gilt Cross, the second highest award for bravery in the Sea Scout movement, for rescuing someone from drowning in the Exe. He went on to make no less than five more rescues, and was award the Royal Humane Society commendation for bravery.

Pat spent much of his working life shuttling between Exeter and Bristol, where he worked for Brecknell, Dalmon and Rogers until 1965, when he finally moved back to Devon. Pat put back into water sports as much as he took out. He was a qualified Crewman and Day Skipper under the terms of the RYA, and was much missed after he final ended his involvement.

Owen Burridge (1929-2012)

Owen was President in 1987-88 and was a longstanding, influential and popular member of the club, renowned for both his rowing and technical skills. It was said that Owen, like his contemporary Pat Smart, could make or repair anything in metal, wood or plastic, skills which he put to good use in the boathouse to the club's advantage. As an oarsman in the 1940 and 50s, he and Pat Smart were often together in a boat, and they projected a good image of the club far and wide, never moreso than in 1955 when as part of the West of England crew, they won the National Senior Eights championship and were awarded the Lord Desborough Cup.

Photo 7: Owen Burridge (Left)

Denzil and Wyn Hitt

Denzil, currently the oldest surviving member of the club, joined as a rower in 1954, having moved to Exeter eight years earlier. His first race was for the U-18s; he then rowed for the U-20s before being called up for National Service, from which he returned in 1958, and rowed as a Junior until 1962.

Photo 8: Denzil Hitt at stroke

Denzil and Brian Sculpher always did well in the pairs, but never won the South Coast championship, so the powers that be allowed them, as a good will gesture, to row in a mixed junior/senior four. As a result, in 1962 they won the south coast junior/senior championship. From then on, he rowed as a senior until 1992, at the age of 56, when he retired from active rowing after 38 years. His grandsons are still rowing.

Wyn was social secretary at the club for 10 years, not a rower herself but married to Denzil Hitt who was and with children who went on to row as well. She was President in 2001-02 and is the person responsible for the president, captain and chairman boards in the club house. As a fundraiser Wyn arranged jumble sales which were a great hit, not only from the money raising point of view but also gave the men the chance to cross dress! She was also actively involved with the search for a new premises and fundraising for that. Ros and Wyn both remember accompanying Brian and Denzil to regattas and dinners etc and then doing the same with their children. Both now have grandchildren who row at the club and it shows that behind the notable names at the club are patient families.

M.T. (Mike) Baker

Mike joined the club as an already consummate oarsman, and quickly made his mark as part of the WEARA Senior A championship crew. Mike was President of the club in 1976-77 and again in 1994-95, and President of WEARA in 1989. His management and financial skills were made readily available to the club over his years in office. New boats and equipment often arrived at the club following Mike's direct financial involvement. Mike Baker was also a Chairman of the Club for many years and Chairman of the City Of Exeter Regatta Committee for 20 years.

Geoffrey Pring

In March 1966, Geoffrey Pring, a long time member of the club, created a Trust with an initial donation of £5,000. The purpose of the Trust was to provide capital for the acquisition of club premises or to use income towards the provision of club equipment. The Trust is managed by four Trustees; the fact that it is now more than ten times the original donation is a measure of both the skill of the trustees and the Club's prudent requests for assistance.

D D Macklin (David)

David joined the club on moving to the Exeter area to work. His pedigree is substantial as a winning Cambridge Blue and International oarsman. His impact on the club both in and out of boats was immense; he was president in 1981-82, and produced improvements in technique which greatly strengthened the club. He rowed in Senior A crews which won Championships in the 1970s.

N J Parkin (Nick)

Nick joined the club as a first class oarsman, achievements at Exeter including being a member of the crew which won the South Coast championship for Junior/Senior Fours in 1962. Nick also made a major contribution to the management of rowing in the West Country. His significant involvement in WEARA produced much needed change in the rules and rowing arrangements which left the West of England much closer to their fellow oarsmen in the rest of the country.

...AND NOW...

The following current members have talked to us about their time with ERC. All are still active in various capacities, and all are highly respected within the membership. Their dedication deserves recognition.

BRIAN SCULPHER

Brian started rowing with the club in 1956 at the age of 23, though he had already had success with the Sea Scouts, rowing in a 'whaler' in the 1947 regatta against the Sea Cadets. He was part of the victorious crew in the South Coast Championships in 1962, and also rowed during the visit to Rennes

Photo 9: Brian Sculpher

in 1962, when in a pair with Mike Baker (coxed by Ray Grigg) they managed somehow to overtake the French boat under the road tunnel in the city centre and won the race. Rumour has it that the cox said something to the stroke man which caused a sudden burst of energy and rate. (What Ray actually said to Mike Baker as they entered the tunnel was, *'stop smiling and row!'*)

Brian formed a formidable pairing with Denzil Hitt in the early 1960s, when they won virtually every race they entered, rowing in a 36ft four with the bow and stroke riggers removed. He also rowed in eights, completing the Boston Marathon three times, once in a coxless four and twice in an eight. On one of these occasions, while returning to Exeter with the boats on the trailer, the towing vehicle and trailer jack-knifed and hit the central reservation; amazingly, though all the straps holding the boats to the trailer were broken, the boats were undamaged.

He also tells of the time they went to London Rowing Club for the Head of the River in a VW camping van, with six of the crew sleeping in it. In the morning before the race, the police came to move them on as they were illegally parked; but as they were cooking breakfast at the time, they offered the officers bacon sandwiches. In the end, having been well fed, the police put cones round their van and left it for the rest of the day while the Exeter crew rowed!

Brian also rowed in the first ever Exeter Head of River race, which started in the canal basin, went via Double Locks and Topsham lock to the river, and then on to Exmouth Lifeboat station. This proved complicated, the clocks having to be stopped and started at the locks, so in subsequent years, the race began at Topsham. In the last ever Head of the Exe, Len Rey forgot about adjusting for British Summer Time when he consulted the tide tables: this meant that the tide went out an hour earlier than planned, so that the men's boats taking a direct line down the estuary found themselves aground. The women, cleverly, stuck to the main channel and won.

Brian has been a stalwart member of the club for over 60 years, as a Committee member for most of that time, Captain twice, in 1967-68 and 1973-74, as well as President in 1991-92. He feels that the club is currently in great shape with lots of young rowers full of enthusiasm and everyone socially active. The biggest change during Brian's time with the club, he thinks, has been the opening of the new clubhouse, which allowed for social events and encouraged all members, young and old, to get to know each other better.

Brian met his wife Ros at the Port Royal whilst rowing, and told her early on in their relationship that she wouldn't see him on Tuesdays, Thursday and Sunday mornings. They are, of course, still here together after all those years. And rowing continues in the family: their son Christian won the U-16 WEARA championship in 1991, and now their granddaughter Molly Bachelor, 14, is learning to row. Brian is deeply grateful to the club for all the friendship that it has offered him, and looks forward optimistically to the future.

Photo 10: Ray Grigg

RAY GRIGG

Ray started rowing in 1958 as a 17 year-old, with three others from school, and rowed regularly until his mid-twenties, starting again in 1991 with the creation of the 'Saga Boat Squad', a collection of the more mature oarsmen who continue to go out on the river. He was treasurer for five years from 1968-73, and Regatta Secretary for 18 years in the 1970s and 80s. He was heavily involved in the planning and managing of the move to the current premises; as he worked for Devon County Council at the time, he was very aware of the issues, and realised it made sense for what were then the three water sports clubs to come together in this venture. The Dragon Boat Racers joined later. He was President of the club in 1991, and is so again now. Over his period of involvement with the Club, one major development, in his opinion, has been the change in attitudes to training. A few decades ago, this involved rowing three times a week and going to the pub afterwards; while now, the crews are training almost every day, on the ergos, with weights and doing circuits as well as working in boats. He also noted how boats and equipment have become incredibly expensive. In the early decades of the club, boats cost less than £100, now they are in four or five figures. And they are no longer, he feels, seen as precious items to be cherished, but as 'consumables' to be bought and disposed of. The last wooden four the club owned was sold to Exmouth club, he noted with some sadness.

Like others in the club, he pointed out that fortunes have fluctuated, from times when hardly anybody went on the water, to the present situation where it is hard to cope with the numbers wanting to row, simply through a shortage of boats, storage space and coaches. He had always supported the establishment of an 'Emergency Fund' to cover those harder times when the club was going through a lean patch. And ten years ago, it was clear that people would have to pay more for their membership if they wanted decent gear to row in and to use. This is why membership seems high.

But despite the ups and downs, Ray still sees rowing as 'a team sport beyond compare' in terms of the collaborative spirit and working together that it generates. I asked him what shape he thinks the club is in currently, and he explained that the problems were, in a sense, good problems to have, such as the popularity of rowing, leading to the need to generate a consistently strong organisation that will continue to move the club forward. The people, he told me, are there; and the way the four water sports clubs have grown and worked together is something to be proud of.

Success in the future, he thinks, is about creating winning crews, as well as making sure individuals achieve their own potential. And as a former treasurer, he also reminded all of us that the club has to generate income to guarantee these things can continue.

PAUL WILSON

Paul started rowing whilst at school in Gloucestershire, then continued rowing in the ERC U-18 squad, gradually moving up to other crews until he retired from active rowing in 2009 to concentrate on coaching, after having his hip replacement. He graduated from Portsmouth University in 1974, and in October that year became Club Captain. This was at a time when the club was experiencing lots of success, especially in 1976, when both Senior A and Senior B crews were WEARA champions, and most rowers in the club were winning in different competitions. They also had their best ever result in the Head of the River that year, with the eight coming 69th and the fours 22nd and 42nd respectively.

The club has been building on this success ever since, he feels, with several men's senior eights victories. However, when the club had to vacate the Port Royal, as described earlier, and work from temporary bases on the quay and in the cellars, there were some 'quiet years'. Success and popularity only really returned when the club moved into its new current boathouse. The late 1980s and early 1990s were again years of success, in both the men's and women's squads. In recent years, the women's squad in particular has been

Photo 11: Paul Wilson

very successful.

The ebbing and flowing of success, he felt, is fairly normal, but might also be due to the tendency now for young rowers to leave Exeter to go to university elsewhere. In the past, few rowers were graduates; but these days, most of those who join the club as juniors go on to university to take degrees. This takes them away from the club for long periods of the year, when many row elsewhere. However, in recent years, the successes of the GB squads in the Olympics and world championships, and especially the much more frequent TV coverage of these rowing events, has raised interest in the sport and brought more people into rowing. In the last few years, the junior squads have developed considerably, with now over 40 juniors on the books: in former years, there were often not enough juniors to make up a squad, whereas now there are lots of young people wanting to row.

Paul also noticed that the 'class divide' in rowing was much more evident in the old days than it is now. Then, it was professional men on the one side, manual workers on the other, whilst now, a club like ERC is made up of people of all ages, a good mix of men and women, and people from all backgrounds rowing together. The club is keen to develop young rowers, and talks to schools about this, though the logistics are not always easy. Most juniors who join the club are here because they have emailed to show an interest, not through school recruitment. Hopefully, however, many of these juniors will feed into the senior crews. The future, he feels, looks good for the club: strong men's and women's squads, and a good batch of juniors.

KEVIN DENTITH

Kevin was Captain from 1992-97, Chairman from 1998-2005, and Captain again from 2005-2007. He is a long standing member of the club and has held many of the club offices as well as being actively involved with British Rowing, by whom he was awarded the Coach of the Year Award in 2003 and the Medal of Merit for outstanding contribution to the sport in 2012.

Kevin joined the club on regatta day in July 1975. He met with Paul Wilson on the day, mentioned that he'd rowed before and subsequently found himself stroking the under 20s eight which beat Totnes and so began a long relationship with Exeter Rowing Club. After a break from the club from 1981, Kevin returned in 1991 and became Captain the following year, a post he held for seven years in all. One notable memory is that in 1996, Exeter Rowing Club won most of the WEARA championships and three of the South Coast Championships at Bideford, which helped WEARA win the Bass Shield.

Kevin coached Harriet Rawlings who won the British indoor championships in 2003 and Melanie Moore who won the British Indoor Championships and World Indoor Championships for lightweight women. He also coached the women's quad who reached the semi-finals of Women's Henley and came 4th in the final of the National Championships of 2003. The crew consisted of Harriet Rawlings, Paula Bowden, Rachel Painter and Melanie Moore.

In the 1990s Exeter Rowing Club became the centre of coaching in the Western region, and since then, over 200 instructors and coaches have been trained at the club.

Photo 12: Kevin Dentith

In 2006, the senior A squad were stripped of the championship at the final regatta of the season: this ended in a fight. On the positive, side Ian Dryden won the home countries in the same year. And on the social side, he had many vivid memories of the 'Captain's Bashes' which were held in the boat shed. These were all-male events, and were themed so that fancy dress was the order of the day, memorable years being those that included an Arabian Nights theme and a Medieval Banquet theme.

Kevin also mentioned a rugby team, The Wets, which was formed from the rowing, canoe and diving clubs. They played for 2 seasons including a tour of Guernsey. Unfortunately it appeared that Guernsey were expecting the 'proper' Exeter club team (now the Chiefs!) and as such fielded their first teams. The tour ended with Wets 0 Guernsey 66 and Wets 3 Jersey 70.

In 2007 there were 6 weddings of people who had met at the club.

ANNETTE DENTITH

I have always participated in sports- athletics, tennis, hockey- but rowing wasn't on my radar until I met Kevin, who was returning to rowing having been successful with ERC in the 1970s. It was the early 90s and the club was in a 'quiet' phase. But with Kevin leading and a crowd of enthusiastic 20-30 somethings around him and support from the ever-present wise "elders", the club began to evolve and experience one of its most successful and active stages for some time. So I have fond memories of Exeter Rowing Club.

For me, it was exciting to start a new sport, but little did I know what I was letting myself in for – after learning the basics, which isn't easy or quick, you rapidly become fully immersed, dedicated and committed to your crew and ERC to the exclusion of everything else. We were soon training at least 6 times a week in rain, sun or wind and sometimes at 6am to fit in with people on night shifts! Saturdays and Sundays were taken up rowing all morning then sleeping and eating doughnuts in the afternoons.

There were tears, tantrums and agonies but there was also joy, happiness and ecstasy. Most of all we laughed a lot. Our crew of Katie, Kerry, Georgie (and then Juliette) with Susie coxing and Alan coaching became more proficient and we began winning races. In the end we won Senior A in '93, '94, '96, '97 and 2000 and South Coasts in '94 and '96. In the midst of this, we were able to persuade the club that we needed a carbon boat in a women's size; so much as we loved the Pam Baker and our wooden blades, by the time we came 5th at the National Championships we had all the appropriate modern equipment. We had also gained Neil (Hitt) and Oggie (Pete Hogden) as our 'finishing' coaches.

Our crew was followed by a succession of talented women's crews which included Julie, Gerry, Emma and Amanda; CL, Sarch, Vanessa and Rachel, and then Paula, Katie and Emma and many others. If I remember rightly, I was the first Women's Captain and I was also Race Entry Secretary. During this period there were equal numbers of men and women in the club, with ERC winning nearly every Victor Ludorum in one year. ERC was an exciting and uplifting place to spend your time. There was great inter-crew rivalry but we also rowed together and had a tremendous social life, thanks to Kevin and a number of excellent social secretaries, including Matt Trevett and Tim Burling.

We trained hard and we played hard. Socially, I remember skiing holidays together, trips to Lundy, ergo racing in leopard-skin underwear, every Captain's bash including the original Medieval Banquet, painting the club VW bus green (it was red) in the rain and travelling everywhere in it, and Alasdair and Ben sleeping in the car in life jackets to keep themselves warm.

In terms of rowing, the highlights for me were competing in the Boston Marathon in pairs, coxed fours and eights; feeling sick after weight training on Wednesday nights; coming 4th in the National Ergo Championships; winning, winning, winning! (sorry but it's not the taking part!); beating Bideford Reds, any time; Katie and I beating some of the men in a pairs race; rowing with girls from Torquay and Falmouth at the

World Masters in Prague; rowing as a pair in a four – only in WEARA!; Pete Woodthorpe coxing us to a win at Hereford and shouting 'I want your babies'; Making Julie cry when she coxed us once and slowed us down at the wrong point.

I had the time of my life at ERC – a truly competitive environment, seriously fit, with a circle of fantastic friends – a whirl of sport and socialising and although I don't miss feeling sick before a race, or rigging boats, I miss the camaraderie and the sense of family that I had in those ten years with ERC. And whenever things seem tough at least I know nothing can be as bad as a 2k ergo.

During this successful and happy 10 years the club was built mainly around young adults and a number of veterans. Juniors weren't really a part of things then, except perhaps as coxes, (Alasdair being the outstanding exception) because we didn't have children of our own and were worried about the responsibility this would require. I know that the club has developed considerably in this respect. Women were always welcomed and I think we made a lot of progress in those years, such that it was recognised that women should have appropriate equipment and an equitable standing in the club. Rowing is a pretty 50/50 male female sport in my experience; long may it continue.

PAULA BOWDEN

I started rowing at the end of 2000, the year of the Olympics (*that* Olympic Four!), not to mention Tim Foster (magnificent hair!). The inspiration from that Olympics created an influx of new members, me included. I'd actually fancied having a go at rowing for a long time but it wasn't until I bumped into an old friend that I did it. And so I turned up for my first rowing session with Angie Hitt (another member of the Hitt rowing dynasty!) and found myself on a Sunday morning in an eight being coxed by Paul Wilson. It seemed to me that none of us had any idea what we were doing, and we certainly weren't doing anything that co-ordinated with anyone else in the boat, so luckily for us Paul had an *infinite* amount of patience.

In what seemed like no time at all I was doing my first race, the Women's Head of the River Race on the Thames, in a ladies novice eight. We had to get up before 6am, it was snowing, we had Kevin Dentith coxing us (not the lightest cox, no offence Kev) and we were very inexperienced, but I loved it! I think that was when the rowing bug really bit. Before I started rowing I used to run, ride, cycle, swim; all very individual sports, so to row as part of a team (sorry, crew!), to be coached and constantly aiming for the 'perfect' stroke was a different world to me, but one that I couldn't get enough of. A lot of the finer points of rowing have always been a bit of a mystery to me, and still are; I've always been of the get fitter, pull harder mindset! I don't think I'm the only one...

There's something special about the friendships formed through rowing. Perhaps it's the fun of going away to regattas, camping and celebrating after the racing or perhaps it's more to do with the adversity, and rowing can be the perfect setting for that, with early morning outings, after work outings, the cold, the rain, blistered hands, physical exhaustion after 5 back-to-back 1500m pieces, long trips to regattas........ the list goes on. But we did it. Not just because we wanted to do well and win (and get shiny pots and medals!) but to do it for our crew, our friends, and to make our coach proud. I've been lucky enough to row in crews that have competed at WEARA, South Coast Championships, Henley, National Championships and lots of other regattas and head races and do well. But to get me there, lots of coaches were involved who gave a huge amount of their personal time; Paul Wilson for getting me (and all the novices) not just on the water but made to feel welcome; Don Fraser for his experience, calm and technical expertise; Alan Pike's quiet patience and eagle eye; Pete Cork's thorough and meticulous preparation (and scary coxing!) and most of all Kevin Dentith's years of enthusiasm, experience and inspiration. I hope that all these people realise how important and appreciated they are.

Exeter Rowing Club means so much to me. Because of it, I've made fantastic friends who are now an important part of my life, I've been able to compete at a high standard, and I've been part of a club which gives so much to so many people. I haven't got enough time at the moment to think about training to row or scull competitively but the rowing bug is still in me. I still get out on the water at least twice a week, with friends, still trying to make each stroke go a little further than the last, and hopefully this won't stop any time soon. Exeter Rowing Club that has made this possible for me, and for that I owe it a huge thank you.

MARCUS BOWYER

I started coastal rowing at Exmouth rowing club at the age of 13, and moved to ERC after about a year as it was the fine boats and racing that I really enjoyed the most. It was great to have support from the very first day: I was coached by Tom Pattichis, with whom I soon became a member of the GB 'Start' programme and became the youngest person ever to break 6 minutes for 2k on the ergo at 16. Most of my early national success was on the rowing machine, but I had also won the J16 WEARA championship in the single scull. I won silver at the 2008 British Indoor Rowing Championships (BIRC) in the J16 category, and then won Gold in J18 the following 2 years in 2010.

I started to get good results on the water too. At final trials in 2010, I came first overall after a long season which started with a few borderline results, then reached the Semi-final of the Fawley Cup and at Final Trials I ranked 1st overall. As a result, I was selected to row in the quad in Racice at Junior worlds when we came 4th, missing out on bronze by just 1 second.

The following year (2011) Tom got a job with "Start" and I was then coached by Jerry Copping. Jerry really helped me grow as a sculler and I dominated throughout 2011, setting a new junior GB record of 5.58.8 for the 2k ergo test in March. Jerry was really teaching me how to row the single; I won the Elite Single at Wallingford Regatta and came fourth in Elite 1x at MET regatta. This was one of my favourite races and I definitely learned a lot about myself; I was racing some really fast scullers (Ben Rowe, Henry Pelly, Dave Bell). Jerry told me before the race to get to the 1000m mark and to push on again. It was 2 weeks before that I was beaten by Luke Moon at National Schools because I slowed down in the second half; but at the MET regatta I really surprised myself by staying with the top scullers (there was less than 1 second separating 2nd-4th) and I posted a pretty fast time for the conditions. I was really confident going into final trials a month later and won by 8 seconds, beating Luke Moon by 12 seconds.

Throughout 2011 I had been contacted by many universities in America offering me scholarships. At the end of the season, I was in contact with Luke McGee from Washington. It had taken a lot to change my mind, as I really wanted to stay in England and scull, but I eventually made the decision to go to Washington as the program that they have was so impressive. They offered me a full scholarship and the rowing programme is exceptional. Since January 2012 therefore I have been at the University of Washington: the first year as freshman we were undefeated winning the Intercollegiate Rowing Association Championships (IRAs) and the Temple Challenge Cup at HRR. Last year I was in the Varsity 8 boat that was again undefeated all year, winning the IRA's and beating Cambridge on the Thames. We raced the Grand Challenge Cup at Henley but narrowly missed out to the GB team that went on to become world champions that same year.

I also represented GB again in Linz, Austria at under 23's. I had been selected for the 4- but was moved into the quad when a crew member became ill. I raced in the semi-final and we came 2nd to New Zealand, qualifying for the A final, the best result for an u23 GB quad! We then raced the final and came 4th, It was really disappointing to miss out on a medal again, especially as two of the guys were in that same boat in Racice in 2010 but I was pretty pleased with the result, especially with how the four was going and the fact that I hadn't sculled since moving to Washington. Jerry must have taught me well!

I am thankful to Exeter rowing club for providing me with coaches and the facilities to learn to row and especially to Jerry Copping who taught me so much about racing and gave me the confidence I needed to be a fast sculler. I really enjoy coming home and rowing at Exeter because it is a very friendly club with so many kind volunteers giving up endless hours to help people like me! Without the club I would probably have never even picked up rowing seriously and I definitely would not have had the career I have had so far.

JULIA WOOD

Julia joined the club in 1994 and has been a full member every year since. She had just moved to the West Country from London and wanted to meet people of her own age. Her first experience of rowing was in a sweep boat at Durham University, but she acknowledges that she only learnt how to row properly at Exeter. Even though she has moved job-wise (to Bristol) she has remained loyal to ERC and continues to race for ERC.   Julia rowed sweep until about 1998 when she started to scull as it was too difficult for her to make crew outings, having a job with long hours. In 1996 she was 3 in the Ladies crew which won the WEARA South Coast Championships and then went on to win the Junior South Coast Championships at Bideford. Exeter had 3 winning South Coast crews that year. In 2000, Julia rowed bow in an eight which came 33rd in the Head of the River, rowing with Avon County that year as Exeter did not enter a crew.

When Julia first joined ERC, the women's section was very strong and that remained the case for about 10 years. The club did not have the junior squad then; there were more people in their late 20s/ early 30s, and that meant there were many really fun social evenings, the Regimental Dinner in the boatshed being very

Julia Wood and Jerry Copping

memorable (ask Paul Wilson!).

As far as sculling is concerned, Julia admits she has been very lucky to have been coached by Don Fraser, Brian Fentiman and now Jerry Copping. In the early years she won many regatta and head races in WEARA, then started entering ARA (now British Rowing) events outside WEARA. In recent years, she has won in Masters' events in the single and double categories (although the latter has been with scullers in other clubs, as there is no one of her age sculling at the same level as her at Exeter). She has won multiple British Masters Nat Champs titles, and holds a number of Head course records in the West of England.

Julia has gone on to more successes recently. In 2012, Julia became the first person from Exeter (male or female) to win at Henley Masters Regatta and the first woman from Exeter to win at the World Masters Championships (in the double sculls). In 2013 she won two golds at the British Masters National Championships and became the first woman from Exeter to win in the single at the FISA Masters World Championships at Varese in September 2013. She also won at Varese in the double with a sculler from Totnes. The only Exeter rower to have won at the Worlds previously was Neil Hitt (son of Denzil) who won at Vichy in the singles in 2003. The photo is of Jerry and Julia with her gold medals from Varese. Julia has been Honorary Solicitor to the club for a number of years.

Over the years there have been a number of people who have given much to the club and who have kept it going. The stand out person among these, in Julia's view, is Paul Wilson, who single-handedly ran the Sunday morning beginners until Sue and Dave Brooks joined. Brian Penn also deserves mention as does Kevin who, in Julia's first 5 years or so at the club, pretty much ran the club with Annette. Annette, in Julia's view, would be one of the most successful sweep oarswomen the club has produced although to date Julia herself is the most successful woman sculler, no doubt to be overtaken as the more talented amongst the juniors come through!

*

The above stories represent the experiences of just a few of the many who have come up through the club to achieve success; there are many others who have had major and minor triumphs as part of ERC crews, but there is never enough room for all of them, and we apologise to those other stalwarts whose stories we might also have told. What those above show is that the club has consistently encouraged young (and old!) rowers and scullers, provided an atmosphere in which they could feel welcome and thrive, and supported them with excellent coaching. And this is the environment which the club hopes to sustain into the future.

ERC AND THE CITY OF EXETER

There has been a long and valuable relationship between the Club and the City Council over many years; so much so that ERC is one of only two sports clubs (the other being Exeter Rugby Football Club) allowed to use the emblem of the three towered castle on their club insignia. This relationship has revolved around issues such as funding, planning, celebrations, regattas and other developments, right down to the present day when a 'New Project' is being planned to use dead land owned by the Council adjacent to the existing clubhouse to create a new headquarters for the Water Sports Association.

However, things have not always gone smoothly! As far back as 1892, there was concern over the Double Locks and Countess Wear bridges; it was stated that the Council will not do anything owing to the cost, but the Exeter surveyor could do the work needed for £55 'if the members of the Club would subscribe five shillings each'. And in 1896, it was resolved that the City Surveyor be written to with respect to the weed in the canal, a problem still faced today. However, in 1905, records show that the Honorary Secretary of the club be instructed to write to the Town Clerk thanking the Council for the "splendid improvements that have been carried out at Double Locks".

A year later, it was resolved that the club's representatives should see Mr. Moulding, the City Surveyor, and point out to him the condition of the trolley which runs on the lines at Double Locks. However, it was not until four years later that a letter received from the City Surveyor stated that the Council would '*carry out some improvements*' to the landing stages at Double Locks, as requested.

Few records exist over the period of WW1 as the club was largely inactive. But in 1929, a letter was read at Committee from the City Education Office warning that the Club was infringing a bye law '*by keeping boys away from school to act as coxswains at regattas*'.

In June 1955, thanks to effective liaison between the Club and school, the education authority gave approval for rowing by the pupils of the Episcopal School and training at the club commenced. The 'Exeter Festival of Sport' two years later generated various initiatives, one of which was an invitation to both St. Luke's and the University of Exeter boat clubs to take part in this event.

1964 saw the centenary of the club, and this was celebrated by the giving of a Reception by the Mayor at the Guildhall for the Senior Championship

Photo 1: 1964 Guildhall Reception

crew and the Ladies' Championship crew. The following year, a Reception was held at the Guildhall for the Junior fours crew and the affiliated County Police crew, hosted by the Mayor, Mr. J. L. Smeall, and the Mayoress, Mrs. Smeall, together with the Sheriff, Alderman P. Hilton, and Mrs. Hilton.

At the AGM that year, it was reported that "the rent for the boat house stayed the same, while the rates increased by £1.10s 5d. The rate increase came under attack by the Treasurer who stated his disapproval in very strong terms."

In the years from 1966, the Club had one of its best ever periods of success, and in 1970, the Mayor held another Reception for the Senior Four WEARA Championship crew at the Guildhall. Such receptions seemed to have become almost a regular feature celebrating rowing and the Club's important role in the city, and in 1973 the Mayor's reception at the Guildhall was for the Exeter Ladies crew, 'J' Division Police crew and members of the Exeter University boat club.

1974 saw the city organise the River Exe Pageant in aid of Scouts Fund for RNLI. ERC provided several craft for the Maritime Museum. These included a State Barge, Australian surf boat, and a 'Super Silver' boat used in a single-handed Atlantic crossing. The State Barge carried the "Queen" and ten ladies in waiting dressed in Elizabethan style, and was manned by ERC. The oarsmen were also dressed in Elizabethan

2 & 3: State Barge, Queen and Ladies in Waiting for the River Exe Pageant

costume. A flotilla of craft of various kinds escorted the Barge.

In 1975, during April and May, ERC recorded a video tape on Tuesday and Thursday evenings at the Port Royal which would then be shown in the City throughout the first week of the Exeter Festival, leading up to the Exeter Festival Mini Regatta. This was held alongside Exeter Sub-aqua club demonstrations, Devon/Cornwall police crime prevention on the Quay and RAF rescue launch from Mountbatten and crews from Rennes, Exeter University and St Luke's boat club. Canoe club and Exeter sea cadets staged events. The Mayor later sponsored a Guildhall reception for Ladies 'B' crew, Junior 'A' crew, Veterans 'A' crew, Boston Marathon Senior 'A' crew and club officials.

The Mayor's sponsored row in 1976 was in aid of the Day Centre for the Aged. ERC took part using the 50ft racing canoe *'Brunei'* (from the Maritime museum, which had been presented by the former Sultan of Brunei) and manned by 10 "paddling crew". ERC raised a total of £5.10 for "Age Action" in this event. There was a Guildhall reception given by the Mayor and Mayoress for the Senior and Junior Championship crews.

The following year, the Mayor's sponsored boat row was in aid of Help the Aged Fund, and involved a row from Port Royal to Flowerpot and back. Various organisations manned boats, many of which were from the Maritime Museum. The Guildhall reception, held by the Mayor and Mayoress and the Deputy Mayor and escort, was to celebrate the ERC Senior crew who won the WEARA championship. The reception continued year on year, until 1980, when the club had the good news that the Exeter Regatta's future would be secured as a result of a £225 council grant. Ray Grigg reported at the time that *"With the support of the city council, I am far more confident of the long term future of the Regatta"*.

In 1981, a Water Sports Day was held for the Disabled: ERC manned the rowing section.

At the ERC dinner that October, the Exeter Mayor, Mrs. Ivy Johns, congratulated Geraldine Brown being presented by Mr. Roy Baker (E&E editor) with the *Echo Sports Extra's first Personality of the Month*" award to mark her achievements as cox and inspiring her crew to victory.

In Exeter Festival week in 1982, as usual, ERC joined in the activities, this time by holding rowing "tuition" at the Exwick Flood Relief Channel. And ERC participated in Mayor's Sponsored Row in aid of Hospiscare.

More recently, at a 2002 EWSA meeting, major proposals for the re -development of the Quay area were discussed. EWSA were to receive a grant of £3,405 for the year 2002/03 towards the rent, which left the organisation to find just over £4,000. The grant was confirmed later in the year: information had been supplied to the architect and a brief prepared for the Planning Committee in respect of the requirements for the boat house and the social facilities needed. All seemed to be going well: several plans for redevelopment had been submitted. But all were turned down; the designs for the new boathouse in particular were seriously flawed. (Club officials explained that, amongst other problems with the proposals, the design would not allow for an eight to be moved from the boat house into the water!) EWSA finally received a formal notice to quit their premises, and were told to agree new terms before 1st November. The three clubs were to meet as soon as possible. In the event, the plans for the redevelopment of the Quay that had been prepared over several years were never implemented.

ERC and Rennes Rowing Club

Exeter has been twinned with Rennes, the capital of Brittany, for many years, and this has led to many fruitful exchanges between organisations in the two cities, not least those of sports clubs.

1962 saw the first visit by ERC to Rennes Rowing Club. The crew was Brian Sculpher, Ray Grigg, Mike Baker and Mike Curtis. The race along the canal in the centre of Rennes passed through a tunnel; and it was agreed that there would be no overtaking in the tunnel. Boats should emerge from the tunnel in the same order they entered it, due to the narrowness. However, the Exeter boat managed somehow to enter the tunnel second and emerge first!

A year later, Rennes RC came over here to take part in the Exeter Festival of Sport. Then in 1964, a return visit was made by ERC to Rennes Rowing club, where we were presented with a club pennant by Rennes during the visit. In the summer, Rennes sent a senior four crew to

Photo 4: 1962 Rennes visit

Exeter Regatta. In 1969, the Rennes Centenary Regatta was attended by a St. Luke's crew representing Exeter, and a St. Luke's Boat Club visited Rennes RC again in the following year.

The next time a party from Rennes RC attended Exeter regatta was in 1975, led by Maurice Cognet. A sumptuous reception had been laid on for the visitors on the Friday night; however, the ferry from Roscoff was delayed by bad weather, so that the Rennes crews did not arrive until Saturday morning, and much of the food at the reception was wasted.

In 1977, ERC visited Rennes RC on the occasion of their club's centenary. Clubs were invited from Rennes' other twin cities of Brno (then Czechoslovakia) and Bad Homburg (Germany) as well as Exeter from the UK for a celebration regatta, along with many of the most important French clubs, totalling 500 competitors in fours, pairs and single sculls. A cheque was received from Exeter City Council for £50, a contribution from the City Council Twinning Funds for the trip. Exeter finished 3rd in the Eights, Fours and coxed pairs, a great achievement against some crews of Olympic standard. Crews received pennants and souvenir pottery from Rennes club. The delegation was led by Mike Baker and John Ibbett.

There have been subsequent visits to ERC by Rennes RC in 1980, when the Exeter crew ran out of petrol on their way back to the ferry, and almost missed the boat: and in 1983, when a party of ten made the trip. In 1990, during the visit to Rennes, it was planned that Exeter would take the original 1962 crew, now serious veterans. However, for some reason Rennes could not 'raise' their 1962 crew, so instead a 40km row was planned, with lunch half way, which proved to be a serious undertaking for the Exeter vets!

And in 1993 there was a visit by Rennes RC to Exeter. On the Friday the visitors enjoyed a trip to the Devon County Show and on the Saturday there was a row to Turf followed by a buffet lunch there. That evening, a barn dance was held in the Boat House. On Sunday morning a race was held between the two clubs for a trophy presented by Maurice Cognet, which was won by the Rennes crew.

In 2009, there was a 'sports twinning' to celebrate fifty years of the twinning of the two cities. It seems that ERC remains the only sporting club in Exeter that continues to sustain a twinning link with Rennes.

Photo 5: Rennes mementos

LOOKING TO THE FUTURE

Exeter Rowing Club has not only stayed afloat for 150 years, it has continued to thrive despite world wars, floods, economic downturns and losing its home more than once. There have inevitably been times when success has been limited and membership low; but the club has always recovered, thanks to the commitment of many people over long periods. In recent years, the club has been undergoing a period of growth fuelled by a number of factors such as the Olympics, more coaches and some more publicity.

This has brought with it some real success with men's and women's crews, qualifying for Henley and Women's Henley respectively in 2013, for example. There are now far more active rowers than a couple of years ago, and quite a few pockets of success. As well as the crews, individuals are also doing well with Anna Newton training for the GB Junior squad; Imogen Mackie and Dan Wilmington training for the GB Under-23 squads; Julia Wood winning the world vets twice and the singles; Eleanor Burke winning her masters singles category at Henley; and Marcus Bowyer winning in the GB trials then going on to represent GB in the junior doubles in Munich, where they came 4th, as well as in the World Junior championships at Dorney in 2011, where they won the B final.

But success is not only measured by winning cups and championships. The other aspect of the success of the club is the sense of camaraderie generated, and the support given to people who simply enjoy rowing but will never want or be able to compete in this way. The club is made up of the very young to the very old; of experienced and inexperienced, men and women, active rowers, coaches and organisers, even a few who can cook! It is safe to say that the without the support of its members, in all capacities, much of the success of the squads and individuals would not be possible.

What of the future, then? How do people in the club see things right now, and what direction should the club be going in? What should the priorities be? A few key members of the club have given their views on this below.

STUART REDDEN

Stuart's role in the club is as Men's coach, including not only the senior squad but also the masters and novices squads. He is also a self-employed consultant for the club's development, which includes liaison with schools, learn to row courses, and especially rowing projects such as the project to create new premises for the club on the existing and adjacent sites.

Stuart started rowing aged 12 with Birmingham Rowing Club. He was national champion and won national schools medals in singles, doubles and fours at 17, and was nominated for the Junior West Midlands Sports Personality in 1996. He started coaching at university for Nottingham Trent University as women's coach, and moved to Birmingham University as coach in 2004, followed by a period as British Rowing coach from 2005-2010, winning many medals with his crews, including in European university championships each year from 2006-2009. Stuart then became Head Coach at the University of the West of England in Bristol, and finally moved to ERC in 2010.

Stuart is actively engaged in helping to obtain the grant funding needed for the new premises, along with Dave Parsons and representatives of the other member clubs of the Exeter Water Sports Association (EWSA). £70k has already been raised towards the total cost of the project, estimated at £3m. The work involves production of a plan, including surveys, architects work which has been on display in the clubhouse since January, that will be submitted to the council for planning permission. The 'dead land' adjacent to the existing clubhouse will be used for the buildings, which will be on a 100-year lease from the council.

Stuart has had a very positive impact on the club in the short time he has been with us. Membership has grown quickly, perhaps partly due to the 'Olympic effect', but also through his motivational skills and enthusiasm.

As coach, Stuart is clear that the club can consolidate on the success mentioned above. To do so, he suggests, the club needs to make clear its vision of how it can improve further and in exactly what ways. The new home is clearly part of this; but there is also a need to spell out where it stands on such matters as on the one hand, competing and becoming the regional leaders in rowing; and on the other hand, liaising further and building relationships so that the club can be used to develop sustainable rowing every day of the week. One key plank of this, he suggests, should be the introduction of 6- or 12-week 'learn to row' courses for schools:

there are already links with four or five schools, as well as with local businesses who may be willing to support such activity, in parallel with a little LEA funding. It would also involve bringing together and training new coaches for these programmes, from within the existing membership.

One current difficulty, he suggests, seems to be in retaining rowers in the 30-50 age bracket as active members, once they give up rowing themselves. Some of these experienced members could make a valuable contribution to the development of new and young learners, to help increase the membership of active rowers. A further area of importance is the developing of better links between the competitive crews and the recreational rowers, to encourage movement between these groups and further increase in the core membership, as well as a sense of solidarity within the club. It seems that the next few years will be an exciting time for the club's development.

DAVE PARSONS

Dave joined the club and started rowing in 2008, having only rowed on ergos at the gym before then. In his second year, he received the 'Most Improved Rower' award, and now rows with the Masters four, having been Club Captain this year. Dave admits he is the kind of person who tends to get very involved in things he enjoys, and so he soon became Chair of EWSA, helping to push for the re-development of the club site. He sees the London Olympics as having kick-started this movement, and is now pushing ahead with plans, particularly the huge task of fund-raising.

The Project, he explained, is now at the planning and design stage, based on grants of £72k to enable this process. EWSA have an exclusivity agreement with the Council for redevelopment of the site, and proposed changes include the importance of each club becoming a legal entity limited by guarantee. If things go according to schedule and the commercial sector comes up with sponsorship and funding, it is likely that building could commence in March 2015.

Dave's view of the future of the club is that there should ideally be an effective and expanding recreational rowing side, strong junior squads and good masters crews, all alongside competitive squads and scullers racing to win, though the club should not be exclusively about competition. He imagines that the club could expand, in the new era with new facilities, to around 250 members. What this means is that there is a need to improve communication within and between the various groups within the club, e.g. using new websites and phone apps that keep members up to date with forthcoming events and help them to know more about what other groups are doing and achieving. This should pull the club together, so that everyone feels to be a part of the club as a whole, rather than simply one member of a sub-group squad that has its own facebook page.

At the same time, he explained, it is paramount that the club continues to be successful in regattas and other competitions. He has seen huge progress and better training regimes and suggests that a next step would be a meeting with recreational rowers to assess how they would like to develop within the club.

HANA LANGO ALLEN

Over the past decade or so the women's squad has been very consistent in terms of the numbers and results at local and national level. We have had WEARA or South Coast Championship (SCC) winners at novice or senior level almost every year, plus some very notable wins and good placements. After winning the SCC Senior Fours in 1994 and 1996, the squad re-claimed the titles in 2004 and 2006. Then in 2007 came one of the most notable achievements, when an Eight reached the semi-finals at the Henley Women's Regatta and had a close battle with Wallingford who eventually won the event. With most of that crew moving on from rowing to family lives, the following couple of years saw a large development squad competing at various national level heads and regattas, winning many WEARA events, and establishing the tradition of sending an eight to the Women's Head of the River Race every year.

More recently, we've had a very successful programme of transition from 'Learn To Row' courses into competitive Novice crews. In 2010 one such group of ladies won the WEARA Novice championship and then came back the following year to win the Senior C title without losing a single race (apart from a disqualification in one because of steering difficulties). We then focused again on the National circuit, and won a highly competitive IM3 4+ event at the 2011 Nottingham regatta.

Perhaps owing in part to the 2012 Olympics, we've had a surge in membership over the last couple of years, and are lucky that this coincided with the arrival of Peter Cork as the women's coach who used to row, cox and coach at the club but had taken a break from rowing. We now have a group of over 20 ladies, most still at novice status but already competitive at senior level. In 2013 we had very close battles against Totnes to win the WEARA Novice Fours Championship, when it all came to the final race in Bideford and the Exeter Four left the rest of the field to win the race by a distance. And a few months later we went to the City of Bristol Head race to claim the IM3 8+ title for the third year in a row. Despite being a novice crew we set the course record, and were the fastest crew in the region by some margin, beaten only by the Oxford University Lightweights.

From my personal perspective as the women's captain, one of the biggest overall achievements of the squad is consistently having an eight to compete and represent the club at the Women's Head of the River race on the Tideway. Having that race as the main motivation in September, once the fun of the summer regattas is over, we have managed to put a crew together even when there was no coach to guide us, we just got on with it, organised our training schedules and outings, and of course grabbed/begged any coach on the bank that was available. When we didn't have a cox either we would find one from one of the London clubs for the big race itself, and having such people in the boat always turned out to be a fantastic experience in itself.

One such occasion springs to mind in particular, when a cox we borrowed from the Thames Tradesman club turned out to have steered several Tideway and GB paralympic winning crews, and his calls and knowledge of the course probably helped us shave off at least a minute in the race! Seeing how much the ladies enjoy this big international race, and racing against 300+ other crews that include Olympic and world champions, one of my main aims going forward is to make sure that we send a crew every year. In 2014 the squad is so big as well as extremely talented and hard working, that we are certain to send two eights to the Tideway, and will have a very competitive squad at Henley.

The growth of the squad makes the future prospects very exciting. We will continue to contest WEARA Championships and keep on building our reputation at the national level. In 2014 we will be contesting the WEARA Novices and all three Senior Championships, plus a strong squad at the Women's Henley. The bar of our own expectations has been raised, and we have set ourselves a challenge of matching or bettering the successes of the past year, with a women's squad that has never been stronger. It's not just the numbers, but the diversity, quality, talent and enthusiasm of the ladies which will ensure that many of them stay on in the following season and help bring along the new pool of rowers that comes along. It still amazes me that a group of people from college students to mothers with grown-up children, from those who have always lived locally to those who have come from afar, and with so many different family and career backgrounds, can gel so well to go through many highs and lows, 6 days a week, for nearly a whole year. Some might say it's all for the weekend coffee and cake on the quay, but I'd say it's for the love of achieving that perfect rowing stroke and the desire to be the first across the line, knowing that you can't do it on your own but believing that you can do it all together.

ELEANOR BURKE

Eleanor started rowing at Oriel College, Oxford, in 1989, and was part of an imperious ladies first eight. After graduating, she rowed coastal boats representing Vospers at Hants and Dorset regattas, then rowed at Wallingford before moving to Exeter in 2004. She joined ERC in 2009 to learn to scull. Her major successes have been in the past year, when she won the Masters B single sculls at Henley Masters, also qualifying in the Senior doubles with Lucinda Sanders at Women's Henley.

Eleanor's official role within the club is the important but complex task of managing race entries. But her real contribution has been the starting and ongoing leadership of Friday morning recreational rowing, including the 'Learn to row' courses that have been successful in introducing many new rowers to the club (including the author of this book). Her view is that there ought to be a learn to row course at least once a year for weekday recreational rowers, as this would be enough to keep recruitment going at a manageable level.

Her main interest remains within the recreational rowing, and she feels that there must be proper organisation of this side of the club's activity. There is currently a degree of separation between the recreational and competitive sides of the club, which could be broken down by better support for a recreational squad, through coaching and backup from more experienced members at regular "off-peak" times. Perhaps the recreational squad could have their own eight or even an octuple at some stage. Although recreational rowers, Eleanor believes, do not want to be involved in regular competition, they do need targets, such as day trips to other clubs, occasional Head races on interesting water, a multi-day 'tour' maybe organised with other local clubs or even for ERC to host such an event for visiting recreational rowers.

Eleanor's contribution to the development of new rowers of all ages has been considerable, and will hopefully continue to bring on new oarsmen and women who then learn to love the sport. The challenge is to find ways to help such people feel integrated within the larger club structure.

SUE BROOKS

Sue learned to row in Durham, and was part of a very successful Durham University crew in 1969-70. She moved to Stratford-on-Avon in 1971 and joined the rowing club there as the only lady member, but met Dave, her husband, on her first night at the club, the night he became Captain. After some years, she took a break from rowing to have children, and came back in 2000 to coach their Juniors after an Achilles operation. She achieved various coaching qualifications, becoming a level 2 coach and later began an adaptive rowing section in their club. Sue and Dave moved to ERC in 2010 and immediately became involved in coaching the Junior squad, successfully bringing new ideas and a new structure to this, based on what was known in Stratford as 'Project Awesome', a British Rowing scheme for Y7 to Y10 pupils. This achieved Clubmark and brought in lots of new junior rowers to ERC. Sue is now Junior Co-ordinator and has introduced more British Rowing skills training, with about 46 active junior rowers in the 12-18 year-old range.

Sue's vision of the future at ERC is to have a social/recreational dimension to the club, along the lines of Sport for All, side by side with regular competition up country, so as to get more young rowers into national squads. Over 100 went through her learn to row programme after the Olympics, and there are many with real potential now. She also hopes to encourage more juniors into the Rowing Leaders Award, begun in January 2014, so that older more experienced juniors can mentor the younger ones. All this means that the club needs more young members and more coaches, as well as volunteers to co-ordinate, organise and help with grant applications. She feels strongly that there needs to be more parental involvement, especially on the bank supervising as well as helping with refreshments and fundraising.

The key to all this, Sue feels, is that juniors need to feel more a part of the club as a whole, and that there needs to be room and a welcome for those that want to compete as well as those that want to enjoy rowing as recreation. Club cohesion and agreement about the club's future direction is crucial to this. ERC has been earmarked for possibly becoming a 'Rowability Club' for disabled rowers, working alongside the canoe club on this. The club can then be seen as truly inclusive. British Rowing has identified Exeter as a safe venue for this; the club is working with Rhiannon Halliday and Maddie Millichap at British Rowing about becoming the centre for Rowability in the entire West of England. Inevitably, the club is now looking for funding to develop this, alongside the plans for a new base. Various avenues are being pursued, including the New Homes Grant scheme, the Canal and Quay Trust, the Councils and others. It means lots of hard work for Dave Parsons, the Club Captain, as well as the whole committee. But the future looks exciting.

CONCLUSION: GAZING INTO THE CRYSTAL BALL

The interviews above with coaches and captains give us an idea of where the club might be going during the coming years. There are active squads amongst the senior men, women, juniors, vets and recreational rowers; and there is a positive atmosphere in the clubhouse in the evenings and after rowing. What the coaches and captains seem to be saying is that all these groups need to feel a greater sense of cohesion, so that members feel not just part of a club but also integrated with the other members from the different crews and age ranges. Competition and recreational rowing, as well as training and rowing for the disabled in future, are all valued, and this makes the future look healthy, especially if and when the new facilities come to fruition. What do we need to do then, to bring the different parts of the club together? Whatever it is, it cannot be left to a handful of extremely committed individuals: it will need all the club to pull together, which, as our history shows, we ought to be good at.

One thing that has come through in the research for this book is that some things never change, some issues crop up time and again and are as relevant now as they were 150 years ago. Things like funding, use of equipment, club location and recreational/junior members have appeared in the minutes through the years and will no doubt continue to do so as committees and personalities change. It is likely that these issues are not unique to Exeter Rowing Club but whereas other clubs have folded Exeter has continued going. This is in no small part due to the outstanding commitment of some members across the years whether it be through running the club, coaching, welcoming new members or simply supporting the club and its events. The essence of the club and the love of rowing remains constant and hopefully will allow it to stay afloat for another 150 years.

Photo 1: Exeter Regatta 2013

APPENDIX: 1913 MEMBERS

LIST OF MEMBERS, WITH DATE OF ELECTION.

LIFE MEMBERS.

Ross, Geo.	- 1867
Baker, J.	- 1870
Pike, F.	- 1874
Gidley, J.	- 1896
Gould, H. C.	- 1904

HONORARY MEMBERS.

Densham, W.	- 1895
Hamlyn, T.	- 1901
Bradnee, W.	- 1903
Hubber, W.	- 1903
Norman, W.	- 1906
Blanchford, F.	- 1912
Binns, A. E.	- 1912

ACTIVE MEMBERS.

Hodge, A. P.	- 1884
Edwards, A. B.	- 1886
Hannaford, W. C.	-
Sanford, F. C.	- 1886
Rudd, G. J.	- 1887
Mudge, E.	- 1889
Bailey, W. A.	- 1890
Crane, H. w.	- 1891
Pengelley, W. H.	- 1891
Packham, W.	- 1891
Pollard, H. F.	- 1892
Passmore, R. C.	- 1892
Laing, E. G.	- 1893
Pyne, C. W.	- 1894
Pollard, L.	- 1895
Pyne, S. C.	- 1895
Heath, G. O.	- 1896
Heath, S.	- 1896
Lisle, W. J.	- 1898
Dunsford, P. M.	- 1899
Clements, W. H.	- 1899
Holmes, F.	- 1900
Voisey, J. C.	- 1900
Wayborn, F.	- 1901
Pearn, E.	- 1901
Clarke, R. W.	- 1902
Gregory, O.	- 1902
Harding, H. H.	- 1903
McGrath, W. J.	- 1904
Smith, C. S.	- 1904
Way, R. J.	- 1904
Dymond, R. H.	- 1905
Goff, J. R.	- 1905
Norrish, H. C.	- 1905
Pullen, J. E.	- 1905
Comins, A. W.	- 1906
Melhuish, P.	- 1906
Stevenson, W. G.	- 1906
Way, E. C.	- 1906
Adams, G. J.	- 1907
Beer, F. J.	- 1907
Cornwell, H. G.	- 1907
Coles, R. V.	- 1907
Dart, E. H.	- 1907
Fox, G. W.	- 1907
Holmes, W. W.	- 1907
House, A. E.	- 1907
Kent, B.	- 1907
Ross, J. H.	- 1907
James, F.	- 1908
Scott, R. J.	- 1908
Smale, H.	- 1908
Thorn, R.	- 1908
Beale, H. S.	- 1909
Clark, J.	- 1909
Chinneck, A. B.	- 1909
Palmer, S.	- 1909
Shooter, H.	- 1909
Harris, H.	- 1910
Peters, P. J.	- 1910
Quaintance, B. J.	- 1910
Bartlett, S. T.	- 1911
Blanchford, W. M.	- 1911
Caldon, J.	- 1911
Cummings, R. J.	- 1911
Dart, K. G.	- 1911
Davies, D. L.	- 1911
Light, D. O.	- 1911
Lock, C.	- 1911
Read, R. S.	- 1911
Richmond, F. W.	- 1911
Wethey, A.	- 1911
Down, C.	- 1912
Easton, E. M.	- 1912
Harvey, C. C.	- 1912
Clarke, S. R.	- 1912
Way, H. C.	- 1912

APPENDIX: COMMITTEE 2013

Exeter Rowing Club Committee 2013

B. Lewis

B. Sculpher

D. Parsons

C. Green

E. Burke

S. Brooks

H. Lango-Allen

D. Brooks

N. Willmington

L. Cocks

R. Grigg

N. Walker

C. Willmington

P. Wilson

A. Whittingslow

J. Webber

S. Redden

P. Minchell

APPENDIX: 2013/14 MEMBERS LIST

APPENDIX: POST HOLDERS

Year	President	Chairman	Captain	Treasurer	Secretary
1864		R. Southcott		H. J. Dicker	E. Follwell
1865		R. Southcott		H. J. Dicker	E. Follwell/R. Southcott (from July)
1866		H. Tripe		C. Edwards	R. Southcott
1867		H. Tripe/R. Southcott (from Oct 1867)		C. Edwards	R. Southcott/C. H. Slocombe (from Aug)
1868		R. Southcott		C. Edwards	C. H. Slocombe
1869		R. Southcott		C. Edwards	C. H. Slocombe
1870		R. Southcott		R. V. Turner	C. H. Slocombe
1871		R. Southcott		R. V. Turner	C. H. Slocombe
1872		R. Southcott		R. V. Turner	E. S. Lisle
1873		W. Weicht		R. V. Turner	E. S. Lisle
1874		W. Weicht		R. V. Turner	E. S. Lisle
1875		W. Weicht		R. V. Turner	E. S. Lisle
1876		W. Weicht		R. V. Turner	G. S. Hyett
1877		W. Weicht		R. V. Turner	G. S. Hyett
1878		W. Weicht		R. V. Turner	G. S. Hyett
1879		Geo. Ross		R. V. Turner	G. S. Hyett
1880		Geo. Ross		E. J. Rowe	G. S. Hyett
1881		Geo. Ross		E. J. Rowe	C. Horsley
1882		J. Baker		E. J. Rowe	C. Horsley
1883		J. Baker		E. J. Rowe	C. Horsley
1884		C. Horsley		A. S. Rowe	G. Herbert
1885		F. Pike		E. W. Featherstone	G. Herbert
1886		J. H. Lawless		E. W. Featherstone	G. Herbert
1887		J. H. Lawless		F. S. Turner	G. Herbert
1888		F. J. Sewell		F. S. Turner	C. Horsley
1889		S. A. Tucker		F. S. Turner	G. Herbert
1890		C. Mudge		F. S. Turner	G. Herbert
1891		J. Edworthy		A. B. Edwards	G. Herbert
1892		F. S. Turner		A. B. Edwards	G. Herbert
1893		F. S. Turner		A. B. Edwards	G. Herbert
1894		F. S. Turner		A. B. Edwards	G. A. C. Drake
1895		W. A. Bayley		A. B. Edwards	G. A. C. Drake
1896		W. A. Bayley		A. B. Edwards	G. A. C. Drake
1897		J. Gidley		A. B. Edwards	A. P. Hodge
1898		H. W. Crane		A. B. Edwards	A. P. Hodge
1899	Sir Stafford Northcote	H. W. Crane		A. B. Edwards	A. P. Hodge
1900	Sir Edgar Vincent	H. W. Crane		A. B. Edwards	A. P. Hodge
1901	Sir Edgar Vincent	R. C. Passmore		A. B. Edwards	H. G. May
1902		H. F. Pollard		A. B. Edwards	H. G. May
1903		E. G. Laing		A. B. Edwards	H. G. May

Year					
1904		E. G. Laing		A. B. Edwards	W. S. Goff
1905		H. Norrington		A. B. Edwards	W. S. Goff
1906		H. Norrington	W. S. Goff/J. C. Voysey (from May)	A. B. Edwards	W. S. Goff/H. Norrington (from May)
1907		H. G. May	W. S. Goff	A. B. Edwards	H. Norrington
1908		H. G. May	R. H. Dymond	A. B. Edwards	H. Norrington
1909		J. C. Voisey	R. H. Dymond	A. B. Edwards	H. Norrington
1910		R. H. Dymond	H. H. Harding	A. B. Edwards	F. G. Hill
1911		R. H. Dymond	W. H. Clements	A. B. Edwards	F. G. Hill/S. C. Pyne (from Sept)
1912		H. H. Harding	E. H. Dart	A. B. Edwards	S. C. Pyne
1913		A. B. Edwards	E. H. Dart	A. B. Edwards	S. C. Pyne
1914		A. B. Edwards/E. H. Dart (from July)	E. H. Dart	A. B. Edwards/R. W. Clarke	S. C. Pyne/R. H. Dymond (from July)
1915		E. H. Dart	E. H. Dart	R. W. Clarke	R. H. Dymond
1916					
1917					
1918					
1919					S. C. Pyne
1920					
1921					
1922					
1923		J. Caldon senr.			
1924		C. R. Browne		E. H. Dart	C. R. Browne
1925		C. R. Browne			
1926					
1927		C. R. Browne		E. H. Dart	E. Moist
1928					
1929	Sir Robert Newman	P. H. Coates	R. A. Wright	R. de F. Ford	C. A. Scarlett/ W. J. Lisle (from July)
1930	Sir Robert Newman	C. Yendall	R. de F. Ford	R. de F. Ford/K. Tolchard (from Oct)	W. T. White
1931		C. Yendall	W. Dorothy	K. Tolchard	A. T. Hooper
1932		C. Yendall	W. Dorothy	K. Tolchard	S. C. Pyne
1933		C. Yendall	W. Dorothy	K. Tolchard	S. C. Pyne
1934		C. W. Lamprey	W. Dorothy	K. Tolchard	S. C. Pyne
1935		C. W. Lamprey	W. Dorothy	K. Tolchard	A. T. Hooper
1936					
1937			W. Dorothy		
1938					
1939					
1940					
1941					
1942					
1943					
1944					